Free DVD **FREE** Free DVD

Essential Test Tips Video from Trivium Test Prep

Dear Customer,

Thank you for purchasing from Trivium Test Prep! Whether you're looking to join the military, get into college, or advance your career, we're honored to be a part of your journey.

To show our appreciation (and to help you relieve a little of that test-prep stress), we're offering a **FREE *SAT Essential Test Tips* Video** by Trivium Test Prep. Our video includes 35 test preparation strategies that will help keep you calm and collected before and during your big exam. All we ask is that you email us your feedback and describe your experience with our product. Amazing, awful, or just so-so: we want to hear what you have to say!

To receive your **FREE *SAT Essential Test Tips* Video**, please email us at 5star@ triviumtestprep.com. Include "Free 5 Star" in the subject line and the following information in your email:

1. The title of the product you purchased.

2. Your rating from 1 – 5 (with 5 being the best).

3. Your feedback about the product, including how our materials helped you meet your goals and ways in which we can improve our products.

4. Your full name and shipping address so we can send your **FREE *SAT Essential Test Tips* Video**.

If you have any questions or concerns please feel free to contact us directly at 5star@triviumtestprep.com.

Thank you, and good luck with your studies!

Digital SAT Prep Book
2024-2025
2 Practice Tests and SAT Study Guide

G. T. McDivitt

Table of Contents

Introduction..i

  What is the SAT? i

  What's on the SAT? i

  How is the SAT Scored? iv

  How is the SAT Administered? iv

  About This Guide v

Part I - Evidence-Based Reading and Writing................................1

  Evidence-Based Reading and Writing 1

Chapter One 2

  Reading 2

  Meaning of Words and Phrases 10

Chapter Two 14

  Writing and Language Parts of Speech 14

  Constructing Sentences 16

Part I Answer Key..25

  Chapter 1 Answers 25

  Chapter 2 Answers 26

Part II - Mathematics 29

Chapter Three 30

  Numbers and Operations (Pre-Algebra) 30

  Units of Measurement..32

  Decimals and Fractions 33

  Matrices 41

Chapter Four 43

  Algebra 43

  Linear Equations..44

  Building Equations 46

  Quadratic Equations..48

  Functions..48

Arithmetic and Geometric Sequences 50

Absolute Value 50

Solving Word Problems 50

Chapter Five 53

Geometry 53

Chapter Six 58

Statistics and Probability 58

Graphs and Charts 58

Probability 61

Conditional Probability 62

Part II Answer Key 63

Chapter 3 63

Chapter 4 73

Chapter 5 88

Chapter 6 91

Practice Test #1 Reading and Writing 95

Module I 95

Module II 105

Practice Test #1 Math 115

Module I 115

Module II 121

Answer Key #1 Reading & Writing 126

Module I 126

Module II 129

Answer Key #1 Math 132

Module I 132

Module II 135

Practice Test #2 Reading and Writing 141

Module I 141

Module II 151

Practice Test #2 Math 161

Module I 161

Module II 166

Answer Key #2 Reading & Writing..170

Module I 170

Module II 173

Answer Key #2 Math 176

Module I 176

Module II 178

ONLINE RESOURCES

Trivium includes online resources with the purchase of this study guide to help you fully prepare for the exam.

Review Questions

Need more practice? Our review questions use a variety of formats to help you memorize key terms and concepts.

Flash Cards

Trivium's flash cards allow you to review important terms easily on your computer or smartphone.

Cheat Sheets

Review the core skills you need to master the exam with easy-to-read Cheat Sheets.

From Stress to Success

Watch "From Stress to Success," a brief but insightful YouTube video that offers the tips, tricks, and secrets experts use to score higher on the exam.

Feedback

Let us know what you think!

Access these materials at: acceptedinc.com/sat-online-resources

Introduction

Congratulations on choosing to take the SAT! By purchasing this book, you've taken the first step toward your college career. This guide will provide you with a detailed overview of the digital SAT so you will know exactly what to expect on test day. We'll take you through all of the concepts covered on the exam and give you the opportunity to test your knowledge with practice questions. Even if it's been a while since you took a major test, don't worry; we'll make sure you're more than ready!

What is the SAT?

The Scholastic Aptitude Test (SAT) is an achievement test designed to assess what you've learned in school. Universities will look at your SAT score to help determine if you're ready to tackle college-level material. However, your test score won't be the only thing that schools look at; they'll also consider your high school transcript, letters of recommendation, and school activities. So, while the SAT is an important part of your college application, it's only one part of the application process.

What's on the SAT?

The digital SAT has some significant differences from the previous version of the SAT: it is shorter in both length and duration, and it consists of two sections instead of four, each with two modules:

- Reading and Writing
- Mathematics

Exam Section	Number of Modules	Duration	Number of Questions
Mathematics	2	35 minutes per module	44 (total of both modules)
Reading and Writing	2	32 minutes per module	54 (total of both modules)
TOTALS	4 (two sections)	134 minutes (2 hours 14 minutes)	98

Mathematics

One of the notable differences between the original SAT and the new digital version of the exam is that an approved calculator may now be used on the entire Mathematics portion of the exam, which consists of two modules. While most of the exam questions are multiple-choice, you may be required to enter an answer for certain math questions; these types of questions are known as "student-produced response (SBR)" questions. Approximately 25% of word problems require an SBR. Note that some SBR questions may have more than one correct answer; however, you may only enter one answer into the response

field. The majority of word problems are straightforward and contain no more than fifty words. Complex numbers are no longer included in the exam.

Type of Math Being Tested	Number of Questions
Problem-Solving and Data Analysis	5 – 7
Geometry and Trigonometry	5 – 7
Advanced Math	13 – 15
Algebra	13 – 15

The specific math skills that are being evaluated are as follows:

Problem-Solving and Data Analysis

- rates, ratios, proportional relationships, and units
- one-variable data: distributions and measures of center and spread
- probability and conditional probability
- evaluating statistical claims: observational studies and experiments
- percentages
- two-variable data: models and scatterplots
- inference from sample statistics and margin of error

Geometry and Trigonometry

- right triangles and trigonometry
- area and volume formulas
- lines, angles, and triangles
- circles

Advanced Math

- equivalent expressions
- nonlinear equations in one variable
- systems of equations in two variables
- nonlinear functions

Algebra

- linear equations in one variable
- linear equations in two variables
- linear functions
- systems of two linear equations in two variables
- linear inequalities in one or two variables

Reading and Writing

The Reading and Writing portion of the digital SAT also has some significant changes from the original version of the exam. Most notably, there is no longer an optional essay. Test takers will also see a wider variety of topics discussed in shorter (25 – 150 words) reading passages. The content of these reading passages will now more closely resemble what students are being taught in school and will focus on science, the humanities, literature (including plays and poetry), and social studies/history. Each short passage will now be followed by only one question.

Questions on this section will be organized in appearance on the exam by easiest to hardest, with questions that evaluate similar skills and knowledge grouped together. The final question on each Reading and Writing module will concern a bulleted list. Those final questions, known as "rhetorical synthesis" questions, typically feature a student's set of research notes.

The question types in the Reading and Writing modules are understood to appear in the order in which they are listed in the following table.

Question Type	Skills Evaluated	Number of Questions
Craft and Structure	• words in context • structure and purpose • cross-text connections	13 – 15 questions (about 28% of section)
Information and Ideas	• details • central Ideas • command of evidence • inferences	12 – 14 questions (about 26% of section)
Standard English Conventions	• fragments • run-ons • punctuation • pronouns • subject-verb agreement • parallelism • modifiers • verb tense • idioms • diction	11 – 15 questions (about 26% of section)
Expression of Ideas	• transitions • rhetorical synthesis	8 – 12 questions (about 20% of section)

How is the SAT Scored?

Each section of the exam (Mathematics, Reading and Writing) has a possible score range of 200 – 800, which means that your total score on the SAT can range from 400 – 1600.

Multistage adaptive testing (discussed in the next section) is used, and your scores are based on how you do on *all* questions in each section. For example, if the second module in a section is one of higher difficulty, it means that you likely performed well in the first module and do not necessarily need to answer every question correctly in order to achieve a high score. (You should, of course, try your hardest on each question within each module—regardless of difficulty.) If you did not perform well in the first module of a section, the second module will generate questions that are more tailored to your ability, which will allow you to better showcase your knowledge.

In addition to your high school, school district, and state, any schools or scholarship programs that you listed as score recipients in your BlueBook app will receive your scores. Test takers and chosen score recipients typically receive scores within three weeks or so from the date on which the exam was taken.

How is the SAT Administered?

The SAT is now administered solely as a digital exam that must be taken on a laptop (or tablet) at a testing center. There are no at-home testing options, and there is no longer a paper-and-pencil version of the exam. Students may use school-issued devices, their own devices, or devices provided by the CollegeBoard.

The digital SAT uses multistage adaptive testing, which results in each test taker having an individualized exam. Each section module contains questions with varying degrees of difficulty. Your performance on the first module in each section (Mathematics; Reading and Writing) will determine the degree of difficulty of the questions you will be given on the second module for each section; this does not imply an advantage or disadvantage for the test taker.

Test takers will be able to access the following tools:

- a digital countdown clock
- a way to flag exam questions to return to later
- a built-in graphing calculator
- a digital reference sheet for SAT math

The tools can be found in the BlueBook app, which test takers must download before sitting for the exam.

To register for the exam and explore testing center options, visit the CollegeBoard's registration page at https://satsuite.collegeboard.org/sat/registration.

On the day of the exam, arrive early and plan to bring the following items:

- your testing device (fully charged with BlueBook app installed)
- a face covering (if one is required at your testing center)
- your current, valid admission ticket

- an acceptable photo ID (valid, government-issued, has the same name used on the admission ticket, and is original—not a photocopy)

- pens/pencils in order to do scratch work

- an approved calculator (if not using the one embedded in the BlueBook app)

Though it is not required to bring the following items, it is strongly suggested to do so:

- charging cable

- a drink or snacks (for your break)

- a backup testing device

Students may take the exam as often as they feel is necessary.

About This Guide

This guide will help you master the most important test topics and develop critical test-taking skills. We have built features into our books to prepare you for your tests and increase your score. Along with a detailed summary of the format, content, and scoring of the SAT, we offer an in-depth overview of the content knowledge required to pass the exam. You can also test your knowledge with sample questions throughout the text and practice questions that reflect the content and format of the exams. We're pleased you've chosen Accepted, Inc. to be a part of your journey!

Part I - Evidence-Based Reading and Writing

Evidence-Based Reading and Writing

Reading and Writing: 54 questions ¦ 64 minutes (two 32-minute modules)

The Reading and Writing portion of the SAT comprises two modules that each contain questions concerning one of the four following reading and writing content domains:

- Craft and Structure

    o Skills tested include using words in context and an understanding of structure, purpose, and cross-text connections.

- Information and Ideas

    o Skills tested include an understanding of the details and central ideas of a passage as well as a command of evidence and inferences.

- Standard English Conventions

    o Test takers must be able to recognize and understand how to correct sentence fragments, run-on sentences, punctuation, pronouns, subject-verb agreement, parallelism, modifiers, and verb tense.

    o Test takers should also understand idioms and diction.

- Expression of Ideas

    o Skills tested include an understanding of transitions and rhetorical synthesis.

The modules contain a combined total of 54 questions; the test taker will have 32 minutes to complete *each* module (64 minutes total). Each short passage will be followed by one question. Many of the passages will be literary in nature and cover a broad historical range; some passages may be excerpts of poetry and/or plays. Please see the table in the Introduction for a more specific breakdown of the test questions for the Reading and Writing portion of the SAT.

The last question on each module in the Reading and Writing portion of the SAT will relate to a bulleted list, table, or similar item. These types of questions typically concern rhetorical synthesis and may involve analyzing research notes.

Chapter One

Reading

The Main Idea

The **main idea** of a text is the author's purpose in writing a book, article, story, etc. Being able to identify and understand the main idea is a critical skill that is necessary for readers to comprehend and appreciate what they are reading.

For example, a candidate running for office plans to deliver a speech asserting her position on tax reform. The **topic** of the speech—tax reform—is clear to voters and probably of interest to many of them. Imagine, however, that the candidate believes that taxes should be lowered. She is likely to assert this argument in her speech by supporting it with examples that prove why lowering taxes would benefit the public and how doing so could be accomplished. While the topic of the speech would be tax reform, the benefit of lowering taxes would be the main idea. Other candidates may have different perspectives on the topic; they may believe that higher taxes are necessary or that current taxes are adequate. It is likely that their speeches, while on the same topic of tax reform, would have different main ideas— different arguments that are likewise supported by different examples. Determining what a speaker, writer, or text is asserting about a specific issue will reveal the main idea.

Questions concerning a passage's theme may also appear on the exam. A theme is similar to—but distinct from—its topic. While a **topic** is usually a specific person, place, thing, or issue, a **theme** is an idea or concept that the author refers back to frequently. Examples of common themes include the importance of family, the dangers of technology, and the beauty of nature.

Be prepared to differentiate between the topic, theme, and main idea of a passage. Let's look at an example:

Marie Curie was one of the most influential female scientists in history due to her accomplishments in radioactive chemistry. Born in 1867, she dedicated her life to the pursuit of scientific discovery. She won two Nobel Prizes, one in Physics and one in Chemistry.

Her most groundbreaking achievements were her discoveries of polonium and radium. As she studied these elements, she observed an unknown phenomenon for which she would later coin the term "radioactivity." This research would be revolutionary for not only the field of chemistry but also medicine and energy production.

Curie's accomplishments are made even more impressive by the gender discrimination that was prevalent in scientific fields during her lifetime. Curie was the first female professor at the University of Paris. She was also the first woman to become a Nobel laureate. More than sixty years after her death, in 1995, she was entombed in the Panthéon in Paris, the first woman to be honored there based on her own merits. Her pursuits have continued to be an inspiration for women who wish to work in STEM fields.

- The **topic** of this passage is the female scientist Marie Curie.

- The **main idea** is laid out in the first sentence, which states that Marie Curie "was one of the most influential female scientists of all time." This is further supported by the content of the rest

of the passage, which discusses the specifics of her accomplishments and how they improved science and female participation in STEM for decades to come.

> **QUICK REVIEW**: A **topic** is the subject of the passage. A **theme** is an idea or concept that the author refers to repeatedly. A **main idea** is the argument that the writer is making about the topic.

- The **theme** of the passage is female achievement. This is made clear by the inclusion of the last paragraph and the emphasis of Marie Curie as a *female* scientist at the beginning of the passage. This is the concept that is stressed the most throughout the passage.

Practice Question

It's easy to puzzle over the landscapes of our solar system's distant planets—how could we ever know what those far-flung places really look like? Scientists utilize a number of tools to visualize the surfaces of many planets. The topography of Venus, for example, has been explored by several space probes, including the Russian Venera landers and NASA's Magellan orbiter. These craft used imaging and radar to map the surface of the planet, identifying a whole host of features including volcanoes, craters, and a complex system of channels.

NASA has also used its series of orbiting telescopes to study distant planets. These four powerful telescopes allow scientists to examine planets using visible light, infrared and near-infrared light, ultraviolet light, X-rays and gamma rays.

Powerful telescopes aren't just found in space: NASA also makes use of Earth-bound telescopes. In fact, Earth-bound telescopes offer a distinct advantage over orbiting telescopes because they allow scientists to capture data from a fixed point, which allows them to effectively compare data collected over a long period of time.

1. Which of the following sentences BEST describes the main idea of the passage?
   A) It is impossible to know what the surfaces of other planets are really like.
   B) Telescopes are an important tool for scientists studying planets in our solar system.
   C) Venus's surface has many of the same features as Earth's surface and includes volcanoes, craters, and channels.
   D) Scientists use a variety of advanced technologies to study the surface of the planets in our solar system.

Topic and Summary Sentences

The main idea of a paragraph usually appears within the topic sentence. The **topic sentence** introduces the main idea to readers; it indicates not only the topic of a passage, but also the writer's perspective on the topic.

Be alert for paragraphs in which writers do not include a clear topic sentence at all; even without a clear topic sentence, a paragraph will still have a main idea. You may also see a summary sentence at the end of a passage. As its name suggests, the **summary sentence** sums up the passage, often by restating the main idea and the author's key evidence that supports it.

Notice, for example, how the first sentence in the text about Marie Curie states that she was one of the most influential *female* scientists to ever live. This topic sentence introduces the main idea of the text, which is then continued by paragraphs that describe Curie's accomplishments and provide context for

her influence. The final, summary sentence, summarizes the passage by rephrasing the main idea that Curie was one of the most influential female scientists to ever live by mentioning how her pursuits continue to be an inspiration for women who wish to work in STEM fields.

Practice Question

The Constitution of the United States establishes a series of limits to rein in centralized power. Separation of powers distributes federal authority among three competing branches: the executive, the legislative, and the judicial. Checks and balances allow the branches to check the usurpation of power by any one branch. States' rights are protected under the Constitution from too much encroachment by the federal government. Enumeration of powers names the specific and few powers the federal government has. These four restrictions have helped sustain the American republic for over two centuries.

2. In the above paragraph, what are the topic and summary sentences?

Implied Main Idea

A paragraph without a clear topic sentence still has a main idea; rather than clearly stated, it is **implied**. Determining the implied main idea requires some detective work: you will need to look at the author's word choice and tone in addition to the content of the passage in order to find its main idea.

Let's look at an example paragraph:

One of my summer reading books was Mockingjay. *Though it's several hundred pages long, I read it in just a few days. I was captivated by the adventures of the main character and the complicated plot of the book. However, I felt like the ending didn't reflect the excitement of the story. Given what a powerful personality the main character has, I felt like the ending didn't do her justice.*

Even without a clear topic sentence, this paragraph has a main idea, but what is the writer's perspective on the book—what is the writer of the passage saying about the book? Does the writer think the book is outstanding, disappointing, suspenseful?

While the paragraph begins with positive commentary on the book—"I was captivated by the adventures of the main character and the complicated plot of the book"—this positive idea is followed by the contradictory transition word *however*. The main idea—implied or otherwise—should be able to encompass all of the thoughts in a paragraph. The author of the passage initially enjoyed the book, but was disappointed by the ending, which seemed unworthy of the exciting plot and character. It is therefore safe to say that the author of the passage found the book to be disappointing *overall*—not outstanding or suspenseful.

Practice Question

Fortunately, none of Alyssa's coworkers have ever seen inside the large filing drawer in her desk. Disguised by the meticulous neatness of the rest of her workspace, the drawer betrays no sign of the chaos within. To even open it, she had to struggle for several minutes with the enormous pile of junk jamming the drawer, until it would suddenly give way and papers, folders, and candy wrappers spilled out onto the floor. It was an organizational nightmare, with torn notes and spreadsheets haphazardly thrown on top of each other and melted candy smeared across pages. She was worried the odor would soon waft to her coworkers' desks, revealing her secret.

3. Which sentence BEST describes the main idea of the paragraph above?
    A) Alyssa wishes she could move to a new desk.
    B) Alyssa wishes she had her own office.
    C) Alyssa is glad none of her coworkers know about her messy drawer.
    D) Alyssa is sad because she does not have any coworkers.

Supporting Details

Be on the lookout for **signal words** (or phrases), or **transitions**, which help the reader identify connections between ideas and can help the reader rule out sentences that do not contain the main idea or are not the topic sentence. Signal words can describe cause-and-effect relationships, the chronology of events, items in a list, summaries, contrasts and comparisons, examples, and clarifications; they can also lend emphasis. Examples of signal words include the following:

- one
- to begin with
- also
- further
- first (of all)
- for one thing
- in addition
- furthermore
- second(ly)
- other
- next
- last (of all)
- third(ly)
- another
- moreover
- final(ly)

If a sentence begins with one of these terms or phrases, it will likely be too specific to be a main idea and therefore will likely indicate that the sentence contains supporting details.

Questions on the SAT will ask you to find details that support a particular idea and as well as explain why a particular detail is included in the passage. In order to answer these questions, you must have a solid understanding of a passage's main idea. With this knowledge, you can determine how a supporting detail fits in with the larger structure of the passage.

Practice Questions

Satellites come in many different forms, and they perform different functions to aid in everyday human life. Communications satellites are used to transmit telephone, internet, and television signals across the world. Weather satellites study and predict weather patterns by tracking clouds, temperatures, and atmospheric conditions, such as pressure. Navigation satellites enable us to use GPS for transportation in cars, planes, and boats. Furthermore, satellites are generally classified by where they orbit in relation to Earth. There are low, medium, and high Earth orbits; however, there is currently concern about how satellites may lead to "space trash" due to possible collision with debris.

4. Why did the author likely include the detail about the potential for debris collision?
    A) to suggest that satellites should not be launched without proper licensure and permission
    B) to introduce a negative aspect of satellites, which are otherwise presented as being helpful
    C) to explain the various use cases for satellites and how they differ
    D) to provide an explanation for why satellites are launched into different levels of orbit

The 15th-century invention of Gutenberg's printing press revolutionized the spread of knowledge worldwide. The printing press is a machine that transfers text and images using wooden plates and ink. Rather than copying books by hand, the printing press allowed people to mass-produce them. In addition to the reduced workload, this invention led to higher literacy rates and education, as more people were able to obtain books.

5. Which sentence from the text contains the BEST supporting material for the main idea?
    A) sentence 1
    B) sentence 2
    C) sentence 3
    D) sentence 4

Alan Turing's breaking of the German Enigma code changed the outcome of World War II. The Enigma machine was used to encrypt communications between the Axis powers. It became a mission of Allied codebreakers to decipher the encryption. When Turing finally broke the code, it allowed the Allied powers to intercept the messages and anticipate the plans and strategies of Germany. This would shorten the war considerably, as it contributed to the Allied victory in the war.

6. How does the fourth sentence support the main idea?
    A) by explaining how Turing's actions changed the course of the war
    B) by highlighting Turing's dedication to assisting the Allied powers
    C) by demonstrating how difficult breaking the Enigma code was
    D) by arguing that the Allied powers would not have won without Turing breaking the code

Text Structure

Authors can structure passages in a number of different ways. These distinct organizational patterns, referred to as **text structure**, use the logical relationships between ideas to improve the readability and coherence of a text. The most common ways in which passages are organized include the following:

- Problem-solution: The author presents a problem and then discusses a solution.

- Compare-contrast: The author presents two situations and then discusses their similarities and differences.

- Cause-effect: The author presents an action and then discusses the resulting effects.

- Descriptive: The author describes an idea, object, person, or other item in detail.

Practice Question

The issue of public transportation has begun to haunt the fast-growing cities of the southern United States. Unlike their northern counterparts, cities like Atlanta, Dallas, and Houston have long promoted growth out and not up—these are cities full of sprawling suburbs and single-family homes, not densely concentrated skyscrapers and apartments. What to do then, when all of those suburbanites need to get into the central business districts for work? For a long time, it seemed highways were the twenty-lane wide expanses of concrete that would allow commuters to move from home to work and back again. But these modern miracles have become time-sucking, pollution-spewing nightmares. They may not like it, but it is time for these cities to turn toward public transport, like trains and buses, if they are to remain livable.

7. How can the organization of this passage BEST be described?
   A) as a comparison of two similar ideas
   B) as a description of a place
   C) as a discussion of several effects all related to the same cause
   D) as a discussion of a problem followed by the suggestion of a solution

The Author's Purpose

Whenever authors write texts, they always have a purpose. The purpose could be to entertain, inform, explain, or persuade. A short story, for example, is meant to entertain while an online news article would be designed to inform the public about something, such as a current event. Each of these different types of writing has a specific name:

- **Narrative writing** tells a story. (e.g., novel, short story, play).

- **Expository writing** informs people (e.g., newspaper and magazine articles).

- **Technical writing** explains something (e.g., product manual, instructions).

- **Persuasive writing** tries to convince the reader of something (e.g., an opinion column on a blog).

On the exam, you may be asked to categorize a passage as one of the types listed above; this may involve specifically naming the passage as such or identifying its general purpose. You may also be asked about primary and secondary sources.

These terms describe not the writing itself but the author's relationship to what is being written:

- A **primary source** is an unaltered piece of writing that was composed during the time when the events being described took place; these texts are often written by the people directly involved.

- A **secondary source** might address the same topic but provide extra commentary or analysis; these texts are written by outside observers and may even be composed after the event.

For example, a book written by a political candidate to inform people about her stand on an issue is a primary source. An online article written by a journalist analyzing how that candidate's political position will affect the election is a secondary source. A book by a historian about the election would also be a secondary source.

Practice Question

Elizabeth closed her eyes and braced herself on the armrests that divided her from her fellow passengers. Takeoff was always the worst part for her. The revving of the engines, the way her stomach dropped as the plane lurched upward—it made her feel sick. And then she had to watch the world fade away beneath her, getting smaller and smaller until it was just her and the clouds hurtling through the sky. Sometimes (but only sometimes) it just had to be endured. She therefore focused on the thought of her sister's smiling face and her new baby nephew as the plane slowly pulled onto the runway.

8. This passage is reflective of which type of writing?
    A) narrative
    B) expository
    C) technical
    D) persuasive

Facts vs. Opinions

On the SAT you might be asked to identify a statement in a passage as either a fact or an opinion. You will therefore need to know the difference between the two. A **fact** is a statement or thought that can be proven to be true. The statement, "Wednesday comes after Tuesday" is a fact—you can point to a calendar to prove it. In contrast, an **opinion** is an assumption that is not based on fact and cannot be proven to be true. For example, the assertion that television is more entertaining than feature films is an opinion—people will disagree on this, and there is no reference that can be used to prove or disprove it.

Practice Question

Exercise is critical for healthy development in children. Today, there is an epidemic of unhealthy children in the United States who will face health problems in adulthood due to poor diet and lack of exercise during childhood. This is a problem for all Americans, especially with the rising cost of health care.

It is vital that school systems and parents encourage their children to engage in a minimum of thirty minutes of cardiovascular exercise each day, mildly increasing their heart rate for a sustained period. This is proven to decrease the likelihood of developmental diabetes, obesity, and a multitude of other health problems. Children also need a proper diet rich in fruits and vegetables so that they can grow and develop physically and learn healthy eating habits early on.

9. Which of the following is a FACT in the passage (not an opinion)?
    A) Fruits and vegetables are the best way to help children be healthy.
    B) Children today are lazier than they were in previous generations.
    C) The risk of diabetes in children is reduced by physical activity.
    D) Children should engage in thirty minutes of exercise a day.

Drawing Conclusions

In addition to understanding the main idea and factual content of a passage, you will also be asked to take your analysis one step further and anticipate what other information could logically be added to the passage. In a nonfiction passage, for example, you might be asked which statement the author of the passage would agree with. In an excerpt from a fictional work, you might be asked to anticipate what a character would do next.

To answer these questions, you must have a solid understanding of the topic, theme, and main idea of the passage. Armed with this information, you can determine which of the answer options best fits within those criteria (or alternatively, which ones do not). For example, if the author of the passage is advocating for safer working conditions in textile factories, any supporting details that would be added to the passage should support that idea. You might add sentences that contain information about the number of accidents that occur in textile factories or information that would outline a new plan for fire safety.

Practice Question

Elizabeth closed her eyes and braced herself on the armrests that divided her from her fellow passengers. Takeoff was always the worst part for her. The revving of the engines, the way her stomach dropped as the plane lurched upward—it made her feel sick. Then, she had to watch the world fade away beneath her, getting smaller and smaller until it was just her and the clouds hurtling through the sky. Sometimes (but only sometimes) it just had to be endured, though. She focused on the thought of her sister's smiling face and her new baby nephew as the plane slowly pulled onto the runway.

10. Which of the following is Elizabeth LEAST likely to do in the future?
    A) take a flight to her brother's wedding
    B) apply for a job as a flight attendant
    C) never board an airplane again
    D) get sick on an airplane

Meaning of Words and Phrases

On the Reading and Writing section you may be asked to provide definitions or intended meanings for words within passages. While there may be some words you may have never encountered before the exam, there are tricks that can be used to figure out what those words mean.

Context Clues

A fundamental vocabulary skill is using context to determine the meaning of a word. There are two types of context that can help unfamiliar words be understood: situational context and sentence context. Regardless of which context you encounter, these types of questions are not really testing your knowledge of vocabulary; rather, they evaluate your ability to comprehend the meaning of a word through its usage:

- **Situational context** helps you determine the meaning of a word through the setting or circumstances in which that word or phrase occurs.

- **Sentence context** requires analyzing only the sentence in which the new word appears.

    o To figure out words using sentence context clues, you should first identify the most important words in the sentence.

There are four types of clues that can help you understand the context, and therefore, the meaning of a word:

- **Restatement clues** occur when the definition of the word is clearly stated in the sentence.

- **Positive/negative clues** can tell you whether a word has a positive or negative meaning.

- **Contrast clues** include the opposite meaning of a word.

    o Words and phrases like *but*, *on the other hand*, and *however* are tip-offs that a sentence contains a contrast clue.

- Specific detail clues provide a precise detail that can help you understand the meaning of the word.

It is important to remember that more than one of these clues can be present in the same sentence. The more there are, the easier it will be to determine the meaning of the word. For example, the following sentence uses both restatement and positive/negative clues:

- *Janet suddenly found herself destitute, so poor she could barely afford to eat.*

The second part of the sentence clearly indicates that *destitute* is a negative word. It also restates the meaning: "very poor."

Practice Question

Determine the meaning of the underlined words in the following passages.

The Great Gatsby by F. Scott Fitzgerald

James Gatz—that was really, or at least legally, his name. He had changed it at the age of seventeen and at the specific moment that witnessed the beginning of his career—when he saw Dan Cody's yacht drop anchor over the most insidious flat on Lake Superior. It was James Gatz who had been loafing along the beach that afternoon in a torn green jersey and a pair of canvas pants, but it was already Jay Gatsby who borrowed a rowboat, pulled out to the Tuolomee, and informed Cody that a wind might catch him and break him up in half an hour.

I suppose he'd had the name ready for a long time, even then. His parents were shiftless and unsuccessful farm people—his imagination had never really accepted them as his parents at all. The truth was that Jay Gatsby of West Egg, Long Island, sprang from his Platonic conception of himself. He was a son of God—a phrase which, if it means anything, means just that—and he must be about His Father's business, the service of a vast, vulgar, and <u>meretricious</u> beauty. So he invented just the sort of Jay Gatsby that a seventeen-year-old boy would be likely to invent, and to this conception he was faithful to the end.

11. What does the word *meretricious* MOST nearly mean as it is used in the above text?
    A) uniquely crafted
    B) unanimously offensive
    C) conveying genuineness
    D) attractive but lacking in integrity

The Blue Castle by L.M. Montgomery

The thought of her mother's expression made Valancy laugh—for she had a sense of humour nobody in her clan suspected. For that matter, there were a good many things about Valancy that nobody suspected. But her laughter was very superficial and presently she lay there, a huddled, futile little figure, listening to the rain pouring down outside and watching, with a sick distaste, the chill, merciless light creeping into her ugly, <u>sordid</u> room.

12. What does the word *sordid* MOST nearly mean as it is used in the above text?
    A) degraded
    B) compact
    C) welcoming
    D) cluttered

Word Structure

Although you are not expected to know every word in the English language for the SAT, you can use **deductive reasoning** to determine the answer option that is the best match for the word in question by breaking down unfamiliar vocabulary. Many complex words can be broken down into three main parts:

- prefix

- root

- suffix

Roots are the building blocks of all words. Every word is either a root itself or has a root. Just as a plant cannot grow without roots, neither can vocabulary, because a word must have a root to give it meaning. The root is what is left when all if the prefixes and suffixes from a word are stripped away. For example, in the word *unclear*, taking away the prefix *un-* reveals the root *clear*.

Roots are not always recognizable words; they generally come from Latin or Greek words like *nat*, a Latin root meaning "born." The word *native*, which describes a person born in a referenced place comes from this root as does the word *prenatal*, meaning "before birth." It is important to keep in mind, however, that roots do not always match the exact definitions of words, and they can have several different spellings.

Prefixes are syllables added to the beginning of a word, and **suffixes** are syllables added to the end of the word. Both carry assigned meanings and can be attached to a word to completely change the word's meaning or to enhance the word's original meaning.

Take the word *prefix* itself as an example: *fix* means "to place something securely," and *pre-* means "before." Therefore, *prefix* means "to place something before or in front of." Now, let us look at a suffix: in the word *portable*, *port* is a root which means "to move or carry." The suffix *-able* means that something is possible. Thus, *portable* describes something that can be moved or carried.

Although the meaning of a word cannot be determined by a prefix or suffix alone, knowledge of the prefix or suffix can be used to eliminate answer options; understanding whether a word is positive or negative can provide the word's partial meaning.

Practice Questions

David Copperfield by Charles Dickens

There was no noise, no effort, no consciousness, in anything he did; but in everything an indescribable lightness, a seeming impossibility of doing anything else, or doing anything better, which was so graceful, so natural, and agreeable, that it overcomes me, even now, in the remembrance.

13. Which of the following words from the passage does NOT contain a prefix, root, and suffix?
    A) indescribable
    B) impossibility
    C) anything
    D) overcomes

Autobiography of Benjamin Franklin by Benjamin Franklin

I have ever had pleasure in obtaining any little anecdotes of my ancestors. You may remember the inquiries I made among the remains of my relations when you were with me in England, and the journey I undertook for that purpose. Imagining it may be equally agreeable to you to know the circumstances of my life, many of which you are yet <u>unacquainted</u> with, and expecting the enjoyment of a week's uninterrupted leisure in my present country retirement, I sit down to write them for you.

14. What is the prefix, root, and suffix of the underlined word?
    A) prefix: *un-*, root: *acquaint*, suffix: *-ed*
    B) prefix: (none), root: *unacquaint*, suffix: *-ed*
    C) prefix: *unac-*, root: *quaint*, suffix: *-ed*
    D) prefix: *un-*, root: *acquainted*, suffix: (none)

Command of Evidence and Inferences

Having a strong command of evidence means being able to take information that is provided in the text to make inferences and support conclusions. This could include being able to logically finish a paragraph based on the information given throughout. It could also include using data from a table to draw a conclusion about a broader topic being discussed. Developing this skill means being able to identify portions of the text that support comprehension and strengthen answers about the author's argument.

Practice Question

"The Love Song of J. Alfred Prufrock" is a 1915 modernist poem by T.S. Eliot. It is a monologue in which the speaker explores themes of aging and regret: _____

15. Which quotation from "The Love Song of J. Alfred Prufrock" MOST effectively illustrates the claim that the monologue explores themes of aging and regret?
    A) "I have heard the mermaids singing, each to each./I do not think that they will sing to me."
    B) "In the room the women come and go/Talking of Michelangelo."
    C) "Do I dare/Disturb the universe?/In a minute there is time/For decisions and revisions which a minute will reverse."
    D) "Is it perfume from a dress/That makes me so digress?/Arms that lie along a table, or wrap about a shawl."

Chapter Two

Writing and Language Parts of Speech

In addition to the reading skills described in Chapter 1, the Reading and Writing portion of the SAT will also require you to have an understanding of the parts of speech and the rules that accompany them. Many of these rules you have likely been using since you first began to speak, so even if you are not familiar with the technical terms, these rules should already be familiar.

Nouns and Pronouns

Nouns are people, places, things, or ideas. In the following sentence, for example, the word *hospital* is the noun—it is a place:

- The <u>hospital</u> was very clean.

Pronouns replace nouns and make sentences sound less repetitive. Common pronouns include the following:

- he/his/him
- her
- itself
- myself
- whose

Consider the following example sentences:

- <u>Sam</u> stayed home from school because <u>Sam</u> was not feeling well.
- <u>Sam</u> stayed home from school because <u>he</u> did not feel well.

In the first sentence, the noun *Sam* appears twice in the same sentence. (Note that the word *Sam* is a **proper noun**, which is a noun that refers to a specific person, place, thing, or idea by its official name.)

The second sentences replaces the second instance of *Sam* with the word *he*, which is a pronoun. Using a pronoun as a replacement avoids repetition and improves the sentence. Because pronouns take the place of nouns, they need to agree both in number and gender with the noun they replace. In other words, a plural noun needs a plural pronoun, and a feminine noun needs a feminine pronoun. For example, the following sentence is taken from this paragraph:

- Because <u>pronouns</u> take the place of nouns, *they* need to agree both in number and gender with the noun they replace. → **CORRECT**

- Because <u>pronouns</u> take the place of nouns, <u>it</u> needs to agree both in number and gender with the noun they replace. → **INCORRECT**

Pronouns can be singular or plural. **Singular pronouns** include the following:

- I, me, mine, my
- you, your, yours
- he, him, his
- she, her, hers
- it, its

Plural pronouns include the following:

- we, us, our, ours
- they, them, their, theirs

Practice Questions

The Vision Quest is a ritual practiced by Indigenous Native American tribes. During this ritual, the individual is secluded in nature, where they pray for spiritual guidance. They also fast during this time. The ritual is a rite of passage that is meant to transform participants lives as they connect with nature, the spirit world, and _____.

1. Which option completes the text so that it conforms to the conventions of Standard English?
   A) themself
   B) theirself
   C) themselves
   D) them

In Celtic folklore, there is a mythical belief in a creature known as Bean Sidhe or Banshee. The Banshee is depicted as <u>a woman, that is seen</u> as a harbinger of death, and her wailing is a sign that a loved one is soon to perish.

2. Which option completes the text so that it conforms to the conventions of Standard English?
   A) a woman that is seen
   B) a woman; that is seen
   C) a woman who is seen
   D) a woman, who is seen

Other Parts of Speech

Prepositions generally help describe relationships in space and time and may express the location of a noun or pronoun in relation to other words and phrases in a sentence. For example, in the following sentence, the preposition *in* describes the position of the car in relation to the garage. The noun that follows the preposition is called its **object**. In the example below, the object of the preposition in is the noun *parking garage*:

- The nurse parked her car in a parking garage.

Other prepositions include the words *after*, *between*, *by*, *during*, *of*, *on*, *to*, and *with*.

Conjunctions connect words, phrases, and clauses; they are summarized in the acronym **FANBOYS**:

- **F**or
- **A**nd
- **N**or
- **B**ut
- **O**r
- **Y**et
- **S**o

These words are **coordinating conjunctions** and are used to join independent clauses. For example, in the following sentence, the conjunction *and* joins the two independent clauses together:

- The nurse prepared the patient for surgery, <u>and</u> the doctor performed the surgery.

Subordinating conjunctions, like *although*, *because*, and *if*, join together an independent and dependent clause. In the following sentence, the conjunction *because* joins together the two clauses:

- She had to ride the subway <u>because</u> her car was broken.

Interjections, like *wow* and *hey*, express emotion and are most commonly used in conversation and casual writing. They are often followed by exclamation points.

Practice Question

Little Women by Louisa M. Alcott

"Call yourself any names you like; <u>*but I am either a rascal nor a wretch,*</u> *and I don't choose to be called so."*

"You're a blighted being, and decidedly cross to-day because you can't sit in the lap of luxury all the time. Poor dear, just wait till I make my fortune, and you shall revel in carriages and ice-cream and high-heeled slippers and posies and red-headed boys to dance with."

"How ridiculous you are, Jo!" but Meg laughed at the nonsense, and felt better in spite of herself.

3. Which option completes the text so that it conforms to the conventions of Standard English?
   A) "but I am either a rascal or a wretch,"
   B) "but I am neither a rascal nor a wretch,"
   C) "but I am neither a rascal or a wretch,"
   D) No change is needed.

Constructing Sentences

Phrases and Clauses

A **phrase** is a group of words acting together that contain either a subject or verb—but not both. Phrases can be constructed from several different parts of speech. For example, a **prepositional phrase** includes a preposition and the object of that preposition (e.g., "under the table"), and a **verb phrase**

includes the main verb and any helping verbs (e.g., "had been running"). Phrases cannot stand alone as sentences.

A clause is a group of words that contains both a subject and a verb. There are two types of clauses: independent clauses can stand alone as sentences, and dependent clauses cannot stand alone. Again, dependent clauses are recognizable as they begin with subordinating conjunctions.

Practice Questions

Hatshepsut, who reigned from 1479 to 1458 BC, was one of ancient Egypt's most successful pharaohs. The role of pharaoh was usually reserved for men, but after the death of her husband, Hatshepsut took over the role for herself. She presented herself just as _____ traditional false beard and kilt. She did well in her role until her stepson Thutmose III succeeded her.

4. Which phrasing option MOST effectively completes the text while conforming to the conventions of Standard English?
   A) a male king would; she wore a
   B) a male king would... she wore a
   C) a male king would and she wore a
   D) a male king would, she wore a

Pride and Prejudice by Jane Austen

The evening altogether passed off pleasantly to the whole family. Mrs. Bennet had seen her eldest daughter much admired by the Netherfield party. Mr. Bingley had danced with her twice, and she had been distinguished by his sisters. Jane was as much gratified by this as her mother could be, though in a quieter way. Elizabeth felt Jane's pleasure. Mary had heard herself mentioned to Miss Bingley as the most accomplished girl in the neighbourhood; and Catherine and Lydia had been fortunate enough to be never without partners, which was all that they had yet learnt to care for at a ball. They returned, therefore, in good spirits to Longbourn, the village where they lived, and of which they were the principal inhabitants. They found Mr. Bennet still up. With a book, he was regardless of time; and on the present occasion he had a good deal of curiosity as to the event of an evening which had raised such splendid expectations. He had rather hoped that all his wife's views on the stranger would be disappointed; but he soon found that he had a very different story to hear.

5. Which of the following options does NOT include a prepositional phrase?
   A) "admired by the Netherfield party"
   B) "danced with her twice"
   C) "the principal inhabitants"
   D) "on the stranger"

Types of Sentences

A sentence can be classified as simple, compound, complex, or compound-complex based on the type and number of clauses it has.

Table 2.1. Sentence Classification

Sentence Type	Number of Independent Clauses	Number of Dependent Clauses
Simple	1	0
Compound	2+	0
Complex	1	1+
Compound-complex	2+	1+

A **simple sentence** consists of only one independent clause. Because there are no dependent clauses in a simple sentence, it can be as short as two words: a subject and a verb:

- I ran.

However, a simple sentence may also contain prepositions, adjectives, and adverbs. Even though these additions can extend the length of a simple sentence, the sentence is still considered "simple" as long as it does not contain any dependent clauses.

Compound sentences have two or more independent clauses and no dependent clauses. Usually a comma and a coordinating conjunction (*for*, *and*, *nor*, *but*, *or*, *yet*, and *so*) join the independent clauses, though semicolons can also be used. For example, the following is a compound sentence:

- My computer broke, so I took it to be repaired.

Complex sentences have one independent clause and at least one dependent clause. In the following complex sentence, the first clause is dependent (because of the subordinating conjunction *if*), and the second is clause is independent:

- If you lie down with dogs, you'll wake up with fleas

Compound-complex sentences have two or more independent clauses and at least one dependent clause. For example, the following sentence is considered compound-complex:

- City traffic frustrates David because the streets are congested, so he is seeking an alternate route home.

> ### Did You Know?
>
> Joining two independent clauses with only a comma and no coordinating conjunction is a punctuation error called a **comma splice**; it is incorrect, and seeing one as an answer option can help you use the process of elimination.

"City traffic frustrates David" and " . . .so he is seeking an alternate route home" are both independent clauses; they can stand on their own. The subordinating conjunction *because* signals that "because the streets are so congested" is a dependent clause—it *depends* on the independent clauses in the sentence in order to make sense.

Practice Question

The Legend of Sleepy Hollow by Washington Irving

I profess not to know how women's hearts are wooed and won. To me they have always been matters of riddle and admiration. Some seem to have but one vulnerable point, or door of access; while others have a thousand avenues, and may be captured in a thousand different ways.

6. Which of the following lines from the text is considered a compound-complex sentence?
    A) "I profess not to know how women's hearts are wooed and won."
    B) "To me they have always been matters of riddle and admiration."
    C) "Some seem to have but one vulnerable point, or door of access; while others have a thousand avenues, and may be captured in a thousand different ways."
    D) None of the sentences in the text are complex-compound.

Clause Placement

In addition to the sentence classifications described above, sentences can also be defined by the location of the main clause. In a **periodic sentence**, the main idea of the sentence is held until the end. In a **cumulative sentence**, the independent clause comes first, and any modifying words or clauses follow it. (Note that this type of classification—periodic or cumulative—is not used in place of the simple, compound, complex, or compound-complex classifications. A sentence can be both cumulative and complex.)

Practice Question

Dracula by Bram Stoker

I had visited the British Museum, and made search among the books and maps in the library regarding Transylvania; it had struck me that some foreknowledge of the country could hardly fail to have some importance in dealing with a nobleman of that country. I find that the district he named is in the extreme east of the country, just on the borders of three states, Transylvania, Moldavia and Bukovina, in the midst of the Carpathian mountains; one of the wildest and least known portions of Europe.

7. Which type of sentence BEST describes the underlined portion of text?
    A) cumulative-complex
    B) cumulative compound-complex
    C) periodic-complex
    D) periodic compound-complex

Punctuation

Basic rules for the use of major punctuation marks are described in Table 2.2.

Table 2.2. Basic Punctuation Rules		
Punctuation	**Purpose**	**Example**
Period	to end a sentence	Periods go at the end of complete sentences.

Table 2.2. Basic Punctuation Rules		
Punctuation	**Purpose**	**Example**
Question mark	to end a question	What is the best way to end a sentence**?**
Exclamation point	to indicate interjections or commands; to end sentences that show extreme emotion	Help**!** I'll never understand how to use punctuation**!**
Comma	to set apart introductory and nonessential words and phrases	Commas**,** when used properly**,** set apart extra information in a sentence.
Semicolon	to join together two independent clauses (but never with a conjunction)	I love semicolons**;** they make sentences so concise!
Colon	to introduce a list, explanation, or definition	When I see a colon, I know what to expect**:** more information.
Apostrophe	to show singular or plural possession	The students**'** grammar books are out of date, but the school**'**s principal cannot order new ones until March.
Quotation marks	To indicate a direct quote	I said to her, **"**Tell me more about parentheses.**"**

Practice Question

Frankenstein by Mary Wollstonecraft Shelley

These visions faded when I perused, for the first time, those poets whose effusions entranced my soul and lifted it to heaven. I also became a poet and for one year lived in a paradise of my own _____ I imagined that I also might obtain a niche in the temple where the names of Homer and Shakespeare are consecrated. You are well acquainted with my failure and how heavily I bore the disappointment.

8. Which option completes the text so that it conforms to the conventions of Standard English?
   A) creation;
   B) creation,
   C) creation:
   D) creation

Point of View

A sentence's **point of view** is the perspective from which it is written. Point of view is described as either first, second, or third person.

Table 2.3. Point of View			
Person	**Pronoun**	**Who is acting?**	**Example**
first	I, we	the writer	**I** take my time when shopping for shoes.
second	you	the reader	**You** prefer to shop online.
third	he, she, it, they	the subject	**She** buys shoes from her cousin's store.

First-person perspective appears when the writer's personal experiences, feelings, and opinions are an important element of the text. **Second-person perspective** is used when the author directly addresses the reader. **Third-person perspective** is most common in formal and academic writing; it creates distance between the writer and the reader. Whichever perspective, or point of view, is chosen for a sentence, it must be consistent within the sentence.

Practice Question

Twice-Told Tales by Nathaniel Hawthorne

One afternoon in April, 1689, Sir Edmund Andros and his favorite councillors, being warm with wine, assembled the red-coats of the governor's guard and made their appearance in the streets of Boston. The sun was near setting when the march commenced. The roll of the drum at that unquiet crisis seemed to go through the streets less as the martial music of the soldiers than as a muster-call to the inhabitants themselves. A multitude by various avenues assembled in King street, which was destined to be the scene, nearly a century afterward, of another encounter between the troops of Britain and a people struggling against her tyranny.

9. In which perspective is the above text written?
   A) first-person
   B) second-person
   C) third-person
   D) fourth-person

Active and Passive Voice

Sentences can be written in active voice or passive voice:

- **Active voice** means that the subjects of the sentences are performing the action of the sentence.
    - Example: "Justin wrecked my car."
    - This sentence is in the active voice because the subject (Justin) is doing the action (wrecked).
- In a sentence written in **passive voice**, the subjects are being acted on.
    - The example sentence above can be rewritten in passive voice by using a *to be* verb: "My car was wrecked by Justin."

o   The subject of the sentence (car) is now being acted on.

o   It is also possible to write the sentence so that the person performing the action is not identified: "My car was wrecked."

Generally, good writing will avoid using the passive voice; however, when it is unclear who or what performed the action of the sentence, passive voice may be the only option.

Practice Question

The Sun Also Rises by Ernest Hemingway

In the morning I walked down the Boulevard to the rue Soufflot for coffee and brioche. It was a fine morning. The horse-chestnut trees in the Luxembourg gardens were in bloom. There was the pleasant early-morning feeling of a hot day. I read the papers with the coffee and then smoked a cigarette. <u>The flower-women were coming up from the market and arranging their daily stock.</u>

10. How would the underlined portion of text BEST be rewritten to use the passive voice?
    A)   The flower women arranged their daily stock while coming up from the market.
    B)   The daily stock was arranged by the flower-women who were coming up from the market.
    C)   The flower-women, who were coming up from the market, arranged their daily stock.
    D)   The sentence is already in passive voice.

Transitions

On the Reading and Writing portion of the exam, you may be asked to identify the best transition for a particular sentence within a passage. **Transitions** connect two ideas and explain the logical relationship between them. For example, the transition *because* tells the reader that two things have a cause-and-effect relationship, while the transitional phrase "on the other hand" introduces a contradictory idea.

Table 2.4. Common Transitions	
Cause-and-Effect	***As a result, because, consequently, due to, if/then, so, therefore, thus***
Similarity	also, likewise, similar, between
Contrast	but, however, in contrast, on the other hand, nevertheless, on the contrary, yet
Concluding	briefly, finally, in summary, in conclusion, to conclude
Addition	additionally, also, as well, further, furthermore, in addition, moreover
Examples	in other words, for example, for instance, to illustrate
Time	after, before, currently, later, recently, since, subsequently, then, while

Practice Question

Nelson Mandela joined the African National Congress in the 1940s to fight against the oppressive apartheid regime in South Africa. He was imprisoned for 27 years before being released. _____, he went on to become the first Black president of the country and brought stability and peace back to the nation.

11. Which option BEST completes the text with the most logical transition?
   A) However
   B) Additionally
   C) For example
   D) Subsequently

Wordiness and Redundancy

Sometimes sentences can be grammatically correct but still be confusing or poorly written. Often this problem arises when sentences are wordy or contain **redundant phrasing** (i.e., when several words with similar meanings are used). Such phrases are often used to make the writing seem more serious or academic when, in reality, redundant phrasing can confuse the reader.

Some examples of excessive wordiness and redundancy include the following:

- I will meet you in the place where I parked my car. → I'll meet you in the parking lot.

- The point I am trying to make is that the study was flawed. → The study was flawed.

- A memo was sent out concerning the matter of dishes left in the sink. → A memo was sent out about dishes left in the sink.

- The email was brief and to the point. → The email was terse.

- I don't think I'll ever understand or comprehend Italian operas. → I don't think I'll ever understand Italian operas.

Practice Question

From the play *A Doll's House* by Henrik Ibsen

HELMER:

Don't disturb me. [A little later, he opens the door and looks into the room, pen in hand.] Bought, did you say? All these things? Has my little spendthrift been wasting money again?

NORA:

Yes but, Torvald, this year we really can let ourselves go a little. This is the first Christmas that we have not needed to economise.

HELMER:

Still, you know, we can't spend money recklessly.

NORA:

Yes, Torvald, we may be a wee bit more reckless now, mayn't we? Just a tiny wee bit! You are going to have a big salary and earn lots and lots of money.

12. Which sentence contains the clearest instances of redundancy?
    A) *This is the first Christmas that we have not needed to economise.*
    B) *Bought, did you say?*
    C) *You are going to have a big salary and earn lots and lots of money.*
    D) *Has my little spendthrift been wasting money again?*

Part I Answer Key

Chapter 1 Answers

1. D: Option A can be eliminated because it directly contradicts the rest of the passage, which describes in varying detail how scientists have learned about the surfaces of other planets. Answer options B and C can also be eliminated because they offer only specific details from the passage but not enough to encompass the passage as a whole. Only answer option D provides an assertion that is both supported by the passage's content and general enough to cover the entire passage.

2. The topic sentence is the first sentence in the paragraph. It introduces the topic of discussion, in this case the limits of the US Constitution on centralized power. The summary sentence is the last sentence in the paragraph and sums up the information that was just presented—that constitutional limits have helped sustain the United States of America for over two hundred years.

3. C: Clearly, Alyssa has a messy drawer, and option C is the correct answer. The paragraph begins by indicating Alyssa's gratitude that her coworkers do not know about her drawer—"Fortunately, none of Alyssa's coworkers have ever seen inside the large filing drawer in her desk." Plus, notice how the drawer is described: as an organizational nightmare that apparently doesn't even function properly: "to even open the drawer, she had to struggle for several minutes . . ." The writer reveals that it even has an odor, with old candy inside. Alyssa is clearly ashamed of her drawer and fearful of being judged by her coworkers about it.

4. B: Option B is the correct answer because the main idea of the passage is that satellites have numerous helpful purposes for humans, and the detail about debris collision shows that there is also a negative aspect to satellite launches. The author added this detail to include an opposing view of the satellites being discussed.

5. D: Option D is the correct answer because it provides details that support the main idea, which is that the printing press revolutionized the spread of knowledge. The main idea is stated in Sentence 1, which is a summary sentence. Sentence 4 supports the main idea by saying that literacy rates and education increased after the invention of the printing press. This is evidence of the spread of knowledge being revolutionized. The sentence also uses the phrase *in addition*, which signals a supporting claim.

6. A: Option A is the correct answer because sentence 4 is used to explain how Turing's breaking of the code enabled one side of the war to gain an advantage over the other. This is a supporting detail for the main idea, which claims Turing's breaking of the code changed the outcome of the war. The word *finally* also suggests that this is a supporting sentence.

7. D: Answer option C can be excluded because the author provides no root cause or list of effects. From there this question gets tricky because the passage contains structures similar to those described above. For example, it compares two things (northern cities and southern cities) and describes a place (a sprawling city); however, if you look at the overall organization of the passage, you can see that it starts by presenting a problem (transportation) and then presents a solution (trains and buses), making option D the only option that encompasses the entire passage.

8. A: The passage is telling a story. We meet Elizabeth and learn about her fear of flying, which makes this most reflective of a narrative text. There is no factual information presented or explained, nor is the author trying to persuade the reader of anything.

9. C: Option B can be discarded immediately because it is negative (recall that particularly negative answer statements are generally wrong); it is also not discussed anywhere in the passage. Options A and D are both opinions—the author is promoting exercise, fruits, and vegetables as a way to make children healthy. (Notice that these incorrect answers contain words that hint at being an opinion such as *best*, *should*, or other comparisons.) Option C is a simple fact stated by the author; it appears in the passage with the word *proven*, indicating that one need not simply take the author's word for it.

10. B: It is clear from the passage that Elizabeth hates flying, but she is willing to endure it for the sake of visiting her family. It therefore seems likely that she would be willing to get on a plane for her brother's wedding, making options A and C incorrect. The passage also explicitly tells us that she feels sick on planes, so option D is likely to happen. We can infer, though, that Elizabeth would not enjoy being on an airplane for work, so she is very unlikely to apply for a job as a flight attendant (option B).

11. D: Option D is the correct answer because the word *meretricious* means "appearing attractive on the surface but actually lacking value or integrity." In this case, the subject matter is about a young man who took on a fake identity for seemingly superficial, materialistic reasons. Thus, his false identity as Gatsby may look attractive but is not honest.

12. A: Option A is the correct answer because the word *sordid* can mean "degraded" or "in poor condition" when describing a physical space. This aligns with the context clue of the room being referred to as "ugly." The rain and poor mood of Valancy are also used to set the scene of her room's atmosphere. Options B and D are incorrect because there is nothing to suggest that Valancy's room is compact or cluttered. Option C is incorrect because the room's described ugliness means that it is most likely not welcoming either.

13. C: Option C is the correct answer because the word *anything* is an indivisible word; there are no syllables attached to the word to alter its meaning—it does not contain a prefix or suffix. *Indescribable* has the prefix *in-* and suffix *-able*. The word *impossibility* has the prefix *im-* and suffix *-ity*. The word *overcomes* has the prefix *over-* and the suffix *-s*.

14. A: Option A is the correct answer because the root word is *acquaint*, which means "to become familiar with something or someone." This is modified by the prefix *un-*, which indicates the absence of something. The suffix *-ed* is used to put the word into the past tense. Together, the word *unacquainted* means that somebody did not become familiar with something in the past, which fits the context of the use of the word within the passage.

15. C: Option C is the correct answer because it is a quote that is commenting on the passage of time for aging humans. The poet is discussing uncertainty in decision-making, the fleeting nature of time, and how decisions may be regretted or undone in a minute's time. The other quotes from the poem may touch on the themes of aging and regret when put into the larger context of the poem, but option C is the most effective illustration of themes since it stands alone.

Chapter 2 Answers

1. C: Option C is the correct answer because the word *themselves* conforms to the conventions of Standard English. Options A and B—*themself* and *theirself*—are not proper reflexive pronouns corresponding to the subject pronoun *they*; the words need to include the object pronoun *them*, and

selves needs to be plural to agree with the pronoun. Option D, *them*, is not correct either, as it is unspecific and does not refer to the self of the person undergoing the ritual.

2. C: Option C is the correct answer because there should not be a comma after the word *woman*, since a restrictive clause follows it. Additionally, since the subject is a person, it is appropriate to use the word *who* rather than *that*. The word *that* should be used when referring to an object, not a person.

3. B: Option B is the correct answer because it uses the correct adverb and conjunction combination. Since the sentence has a negative function, as the speaker is saying she is not a rascal and is not a wretch, the adverb and conjunction should follow suit. They should match in quality; therefore, *neither* and *nor* are correct. Option C and D are incorrect because combining *either* and *nor* or *neither* and *or* would be inconsistent. Option A is incorrect because *either* and *or* do not match the context of the sentence, which is a denial of qualities that calls for negative words.

4. A: Option A is the correct answer because it combines two independent clauses that are connected in idea; therefore, a semicolon is the most appropriate punctuation. Option B is incorrect because ellipses are not needed, as there is no clear need for a pause. Option C is incorrect because the word *and* precedes an independent clause and would need to have a comma before it to be grammatically correct; it also provides more separation between the ideas than necessary. Option D is incorrect, as a comma cannot separate two independent clauses unless followed by a conjunction.

5. C: Option C is correct because it does not feature a preposition. To create a prepositional phrase, there must be a preposition before the noun or pronoun that reflects the relationship between the elements in the sentence. Option A has the preposition *by* and includes the object of the party. Option B has the preposition *with* and the object *her*. Option D includes the preposition *on* and the object of the stranger.

6. C: Option C is the compound-complex sentence because it has two independent clauses and a dependent clause. Options A and B feature simple sentences that do not have dependent clauses. Option D is incorrect because option C is a compound-complex sentence.

7. B: Option B is the correct answer because the sentence is cumulative, starting with an independent clause and building upon the main idea with independent and dependent clauses. The sentence is also compound-complex because it features two independent clauses and a dependent clause. The sentence is not a complex sentence due to having two independent clauses and a dependent clause, and it is not periodic because the main idea of the sentence is not held until the end.

8. A: Option A is the correct answer because the sentence has two independent clauses, which means that the most appropriate way to combine them is with a semicolon. A comma (option B) would require a dependent clause; however, this sentence has two independent clauses. A colon (option C) is not appropriate since a list, definition, or explanation is not being included. No punctuation (option D) would create a run-on sentence.

9. C: Option C is the correct answer because the passage's use of the words *his* and *their* rather than the first-person and second-person equivalents *I* or *you* indicates that it is written in the third person—not first person (option A) or second person (option B). Fourth person (option D) is not generally discussed as its own perspective within English literature.

10. B: Option B is written using passive voice because the focus of the sentence is on the daily stock being arranged rather than the flower-women who are arranging it. Since passive voice focuses on the subject being acted on rather than the person performing the action, this is the best answer. Options A

and C are in active voice since the person performing the action comes first. The original sentence is also in active voice; therefore, option D is incorrect.

11. D: Option D is the correct answer because it indicates that Mandela became president *after* his time in prison. It is a transition word used to show an action in the context of time. The word *however* (option A) would not work since the text is not contrasting Mandela's imprisonment and political rise. *Additionally* (option B) could work but not as well as *subsequently*, which better highlights the order of events. *For example* (option C) does not work since Mandela's presidency is not an example of anything discussed in the text.

12. C: Option C is an example of a sentence that contains a clear instance of redundancy ("big salary" and "earn lots and lots of money") since earning a "big salary" implies earning "lots and lots of money." The sentence could more concisely be written as, "You are going to earn a lot of money."

Part II - Mathematics

Module I: Approximately 22 questions ¦ 35 minutes (with calculator)
Module II: Approximately 22 questions ¦ 35 minutes (with calculator)

The Mathematics section of the SAT tests your knowledge of math concepts taught through the tenth grade. As with the Reading and Writing portion of the exam, the Mathematics portion of the SAT is composed of two modules. The first module will contain a variety of questions that, in terms of degree of difficulty, are considered either easy, medium, or difficult. The test taker's performance on the first module dictates the degree of difficulty for the second module.

Each module of the Mathematics portion of the exam will contain questions from all four of the following math categories:

- Algebra

- Advanced Math

- Problem-solving and Data Analysis

- Geometry and Trigonometry

Approximately 75 percent of the questions in each module will be multiple-choice; the remaining questions will be "set in context" (known as "grid-in" questions on the paper version of the exam) and require a student-produced response. Word problems will be based on social studies, science, or other real-world scenarios.

Unlike the original SAT, the digital version of the exam allows the test taker to use a graphing calculator for *both* modules of the Mathematics portion. Test takers may use the built-in Desmos graphing calculator on the exam, or they may bring a graphing calculator of their choosing as long as it meets the guidelines set forth by the College Board for use in the SAT Suite of Assessments. It is important to note that some questions may be answered more efficiently *without* the use of a calculator; it is therefore important for test takers to understand basic math concepts and employ reasoning abilities in order to save time.

The majority of the questions will require you to use complex reasoning to work through multiple steps. Test takers can expect to perform tasks like building equations from word problems, comparing expressions, and interpreting figures. In the digital version of the SAT, each word problem will be short (50 words or less) and have only one corresponding question, and student-produced response questions can now be negative and include an extra digit. The digital version of the SAT no longer contains questions concerning complex or imaginary numbers.

Chapter Three

Numbers and Operations (Pre-Algebra)

In order to do any type of math—whether it is basic geometry or advanced calculus—you need to have a solid understanding of numbers and operations.

Types of Numbers

Integers are whole numbers, including the counting numbers, the negative counting numbers, and zero; they include the following numbers:

- 3, 2, 1, 0, –1, –2, –3

Rational numbers are created by dividing one integer by another integer. They can be expressed as fractions or as decimals. For example, the following operation and its quotient create a rational number that can be expressed as a fraction or a decimal:

- $3 \div 4 = \frac{3}{4}$

- $3 \div 4 = \mathbf{0.75}$

Irrational numbers are numbers that <u>cannot</u> be written as fractions; they are decimals that go on forever without repeating. The number **pi (π)**—3.14159—is an example of an irrational number.

Imaginary numbers are numbers that, when squared, give a negative result. Imaginary numbers use the symbol i to represent $\sqrt{-1}$, so $3i = \sqrt[3]{-1}$ and $(3i)^2 = -9$.

Complex numbers are combinations of real and imaginary numbers, written in the form $a + bi$, where a is the real number and bi is the imaginary number. An example of a complex number is $4 + 2i$. When adding complex numbers, the real and imaginary numbers should be added separately:

- $(4 + 2i) + (3 + i) = 7 + 3i$

> **Helpful Hint**:
>
> As of 2024, the SAT no longer tests students' knowledge on complex numbers; however, it is still a good idea to be familiar with the concept.

Practice Questions

1. Is $\sqrt{5}$ a rational or irrational number?

2. What kind of number is $-\sqrt{64}$?

3. Solve: $(3 + 5i) - (1 - 2i)$

Working with Positive and Negative Numbers

Adding, multiplying, and dividing numbers can yield positive or negative values depending on the signs of the original numbers. Knowing these rules can help you better determine if an answer is correct:

- $(+) + (-) =$ the sign of the larger number
- $(-) + (-) =$ negative number
- $(-) \times (-) =$ positive number
- $(-) \times (+) =$ negative number
- $(-) \div (-) =$ positive number
- $(-) \div (+) =$ negative number

Practice Questions

4. Find the product of −10 and 47.

5. What is the sum of −65 and −32?

6. Is the product of −7 and 4 less than −7, between −7 and 4, or greater than 4?

7. What is the value of −16 divided by 2.5?

Order of Operations

Operations in a mathematical expression are always performed in a specific order, which is described by the acronym **PEMDAS**:

1. **P**arentheses
2. **E**xponents
3. **M**ultiplication
4. **D**ivision
5. **A**ddition
6. **S**ubtraction

- Perform the operations within parentheses first, and then address any exponents.
- After those steps, perform all multiplication and division.
   - These are carried out from left to right as they appear in the problem.
- Finally, do all required addition and subtraction, also from left to right, as each operation appears in the problem.

Practice Questions

8. Solve: $[-(2)^2 - (4 + 7)]$

9. Solve: $(5)^2 \div 5 + 4 \times 2$

10. Solve the expression: $15 \times (4 + 8) - 3^3$

11. Solve the expression: $(\frac{5}{2} \times 4) + 23 - 4^2$

Units of Measurement

Some units of measurement are expected to be memorized; these appear in Table 3.1. When doing unit conversion problems (i.e., when converting one unit to another), find the conversion factor, and then apply that factor to the given measurement to find the new units.

Table 3.1. Unit Prefixes		
Prefix	**Symbol**	**Multiplication Factor**
tera	T	1,000,000,000,000
giga	G	1,000,000,000
mega	M	1,000,000
kilo	k	1,000
hecto	h	100
deca	da	10
base unit	--	--
deci	d	0.1
centi	c	0.01
milli	m	0.001
micro	μ	0.0000001
nano	n	0.0000000001
pico	p	0.0000000000001

Table 3.2. Units and Conversion Factors		
Dimension	**American**	**SI**
length	inch/foot/yard/mile	meter
mass	ounce/pound/ton	gram
volume	cup/pint/quart/gallon	liter

TRIVIUM
—TEST PREP—

Table 3.2. Units and Conversion Factors		
Dimension	**American**	**SI**
force	pound-force	newton
pressure	pound-force per square inch	pascal
work and energy	cal/British thermal unit	joule
temperature	Fahrenheit	kelvin
charge	faraday	Coulomb
Conversion Factors		

1 in = 2.54 cm	1 lb = 0.454 kg
1 yd = 0.914 m	1 cal = 4.19 J
1 mile = 1.61 km	1 °F = _59 (°F − 32)
1 gallon = 3.785 L	1 cm3 = 1 mL
1 oz = 28.35 g	1 hour = 3,600 s

Practice Questions

12. A fence measures 15 ft. long. How many yards long is the fence?

13. A pitcher can hold 24 cups. How many gallons can it hold?

14. A spool of wire holds 144 in. of wire. If Mario has 3 spools, how many feet of wire does he have?

15. A ball rolling across a table travels 6 inches per second. How many feet will it travel in 1 minute?

16. How many millimeters are in 0.5 meters?

17. A lead ball weighs 38 g. How many kilograms does it weigh?

18 How many cubic centimeters are in 10 L?

19. Jennifer's pencil was initially 10 centimeters long. After she sharpened it, it was 9.6 centimeters long. How many millimeters did she lose from her pencil by sharpening it?

Decimals and Fractions

When **adding and subtracting decimals**, the numbers should be arranged up so that the decimals are aligned. From there, subtract the ones place from the ones place, the tenths place from the tenths place, and so on.

When **multiplying decimals**, start by multiplying the numbers normally. You can then determine the placement of the decimal point in the result by adding the number of digits after the decimal in each of the numbers that were multiplied together.

When **dividing decimals**, move the decimal point in the divisor (the number you are dividing *by*) until it is a whole number. You can then move the decimal in the dividend (the number you are dividing *into*) the same number of places in the same direction. Finally, divide the new numbers normally to get the correct answer.

Practice Questions

20. Find the sum of 17.07 and 2.52.

21. Jeannette has 7.4 gallons of gas in her tank. After driving, she has 6.8 gallons. How many gallons of gas did she use?

22. What is the product of 0.25 and 1.4?

23. Find the quotient of 0.8 ÷ 0.2.

24. Find the quotient when 40 is divided by 0.25.

Working with Fractions

Fractions are made up of two parts: the **numerator**, which appears above the bar, and the **denominator**, which appears below the bar. If a fraction is in its simplest form, the numerator and the denominator share no common factors. A fraction with a numerator larger than its denominator is an **improper fraction**; when the denominator is larger than the numerator, it is known as a proper fraction.

Improper fractions can be converted into proper fractions by dividing the numerator by the denominator. The resulting whole number is placed to the left of the fraction, and the remainder becomes the new numerator; the denominator does not change. The new number is called a **mixed number** because it contains a whole number and a fraction. Mixed numbers can be turned into improper fractions through the reverse process: multiply the whole number by the denominator and add the numerator to get the new numerator.

Practice Questions

25. Simplify the fraction $\frac{121}{77}$.

26. Convert $\frac{37}{5}$ into a proper fraction.

Multiplying and Dividing Fractions

To **multiply fractions**, convert any mixed numbers into improper fractions and multiply the numerators together and the denominators together; reduce to lowest terms if needed.

> **Did You Know?**
>
> Inverting a fraction changes multiplication to division: $\frac{a}{b} \div \frac{c}{d} = \frac{a}{b} \times \frac{d}{c} = \frac{ad}{bc}$

To **divide fractions**, first convert any mixed fractions into single fractions, and then invert the second fraction so that the denominator and numerator are switched. Finally, multiply the numerators together and the denominators together.

Practice Questions

27. Find $\frac{7}{8} \div \frac{1}{4}$

28. What is the product of $\frac{1}{12}$ and $\frac{6}{8}$?

29. Find the quotient: $\frac{2}{5} \div 1\frac{1}{5}$

30. A recipe calls for $\frac{1}{4}$ cup of sugar. If 8.5 batches of the recipe are needed, how many cups of sugar will be used?

Adding and Subtracting Fractions

A **common denominator** is required when adding and subtracting fractions. To find the common denominator, multiply each fraction by the number 1. With fractions, any number over itself (e.g., $\frac{5}{5}, \frac{12}{12}$) is equivalent to 1, so multiplying by such a fraction can change the denominator without changing the value of the fraction. Once the denominators are the same, the numerators can be added or subtracted.

To **add mixed numbers**, first add the whole numbers and then add the fractions. To **subtract mixed numbers**, convert each number to an improper fraction, and then subtract the numerators.

Practice Questions

31. Simplify the expression: $\frac{2}{3} - \frac{1}{5}$

32. Find the difference between $2\frac{1}{3} - \frac{3}{2}$

33. Find the sum of $\frac{9}{16}, \frac{1}{2},$ and $\frac{7}{4}$

34. Sabrina has $\frac{2}{3}$ of a can of red paint. Her friend Amos has $\frac{1}{6}$ of a can. How much red paint do they have combined?

Converting Fractions To Decimals

Although calculators may be used on both modules of the Mathematics portion of the digital SAT, it is helpful to know the following techniques that can be used to navigate between the fractions and decimals.

Memorizing common decimals and their fractional equivalents (as seen in Table 3.3.) is one of the most helpful techniques. With these values, it is possible to convert more complicated fractions as well. For example, $\frac{2}{5}$ is just $\frac{1}{5}$ multiplied by 2, so $\frac{2}{5} = 0.2 \times 2 = 0.4$.

Decimals and Fractions

Table 3.3. Fractions to Decimals	
Fraction	Decimal
$\frac{1}{2}$	0.5
$\frac{1}{3}$	$0.\overline{33}$
$\frac{1}{4}$	0.25
$\frac{1}{5}$	0.2
$\frac{1}{6}$	$0.1\overline{66}$
$\frac{1}{7}$	$0.\overline{14287}$
$\frac{1}{8}$	0.125
$\frac{1}{9}$	$0.\overline{11}$
$\frac{1}{10}$	0.1

Knowledge of **common decimal equivalents** to fractions can also help with estimation. Understanding common decimal equivalents can be particularly helpful on multiple-choice tests like the SAT, where excluding incorrect answers is just as helpful as knowing how to find the correct answer. For example, to find $\frac{5}{8}$ in decimal form for an answer, any answers less than 0.5 can be eliminated because $\frac{4}{8} = 0.5$. You may also know that $\frac{6}{8}$ is the same as $\frac{3}{4}$, or 0.75, so anything above 0.75 can be eliminated as well.

Another helpful trick is to check if the denominator is easily divisible by 100. For example in the fraction $\frac{9}{20}$, 20 goes into 100 five times, so you can multiply the top and bottom by 5 to get $\frac{45}{100}$, or 0.45.

If none of these techniques work, you will need to find the decimal by dividing the denominator by the numerator using long division.

Practice Questions

35. Write $\frac{8}{18}$ as a decimal.

36. Write the fraction $\frac{3}{16}$ as a decimal.

Converting Decimals to Fractions

Converting a decimal into a fraction is more straightforward than converting fractions to decimals. To **convert a decimal**, simply use the numbers that come after the decimal as the numerator in the fraction. The denominator will be a power of 10 that matches the place value for the original decimal. For example, the denominator for 0.46 would be 100 because the last number is in the hundredths place; likewise, the denominator for 0.657 would be 1,000 because the last number is in the thousandths place. Once this fraction has been set up, all that is left to do is to simplify it.

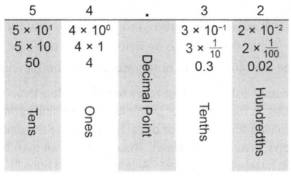

$$50 + 4 + 0.3 + 0.02 = 54.32$$

Figure 3.1. Decimal Places

Practice Question

37. Convert 0.45 into a fraction.

Ratios

A **ratio** describes the quantity of one thing in relation to the quantity of another. Unlike fractions, ratios do not give a part relative to a whole; instead, they compare two values. For example, if there are 3 apples and 4 oranges, the ratio of apples to oranges is 3 to 4. Ratios can be written using words (3 to 4), fractions ($\frac{3}{4}$), or colons (3 : 4).

It is helpful to rewrite a ratio as a fraction that expresses a part to a whole. For instance, in the example above there are 7 total pieces of fruit, so the fraction of the fruit that is apples is $\frac{3}{7}$, while oranges make up $\frac{4}{7}$ of the fruit collection.

When working with ratios, the units of the values being compared should always be considered. Questions on the SAT may require you to revise a ratio using the same units on both sides. For example, the ratio "3 minutes to 7 seconds" would be revised as "180 seconds to 7 seconds" in order to ensure that the same units are used on either side of the ratio.

Practice Questions

38. There are 90 voters in a room, and each is either a Democrat or a Republican. The ratio of Democrats to Republicans is $5:4$. How many Republicans are there?

39. The ratio of students to teachers in a school is $15:1$. If there are 38 teachers, how many students attend the school?

Proportions

A **proportion** is an equation that equates two ratios. Proportions are usually written as two fractions joined by an equal sign ($\frac{a}{b} = \frac{c}{d}$), but they can also be written using colons ($a:b::c:d$). Note that in a proportion, the units must be the same in both numerators and in both denominators.

Questions on the SAT may involve asking the test taker to find the fourth value of a proportion after being given three of the values. In these types of problems, the missing variable can be solved for by **cross multiplying** (i.e., multiplying the numerator of each fraction by the denominator of the other to get an equation with no fractions, as shown below). The equation can then be solved using basic algebra. (For more on solving basic equations, see "Algebraic Expressions.")

$$\frac{a}{b} = \frac{c}{d} \rightarrow ad = bc$$

Practice Questions

40. A train traveling 120 miles takes 3 hours to get to its destination. How long will it take for the train to travel 180 miles?

41. One acre of wheat requires 500 gallons of water. How many acres can be watered with 2600 gallons?

42. If $35:5::49:x$, find x.

Percentages

A **percent** is the ratio of a part to the whole. Questions may give the part and the whole and ask for the percent, or give the percent and the whole and ask for the part, or give the part and the percent and ask for the value of the whole. The equation for percentages can be rearranged to solve for any of these:

- $percent = \frac{part}{whol}$
- $part = whole \times percent$
- $whole = \frac{part}{percent}$

In the equations above, the percent should always be expressed as a decimal. In order to convert a decimal into a percentage value, simply multiply it by 100. For example, if

> **Did You Know?**
>
> Seeing the word *of* usually indicates the whole that appears in the problem. For example, a problem might say, "Ella ate 2 slices of the pizza," which means that the pizza is the whole.

someone reads 5 pages (the part) of a 10-page article (the whole), that person has read $\frac{5}{10} = .50$ or 50%. [The percent sign (%) is used once the decimal has been multiplied by 100.]

Note that when solving these problems, the units for the part and the whole should be the same. For example, if someone reading a book says that she has read 5 pages out of 15 chapters, it does not make any sense; however, saying that someone has read 5 chapters out of 15 chapters, for instance, would make sense.

Practice Questions

43. 45 is 15% of what number?

44. Jim spent 30% of his paycheck at the fair. He spent $15 for a hat, $30 for a shirt, and $20 playing games. How much was his paycheck? (Round to the nearest dollar.)

45. What percent of 65 is 39?

46. Greta and Max sell cable subscriptions. In a given month, Greta sells 45 subscriptions and Max sells 51. If 240 total subscriptions were sold during that month, what percentage were NOT sold by Greta or Max?

47. Grant needs to score 75% on an exam. If the exam has 45 questions, AT LEAST how many does Grant need to answer correctly to get this score?

Percent Change

Percent change problems ask you to calculate how much a given quantity has changed. The problems are solved in a similar way to regular percent problems, except that the amount of change is used instead of the part. Note that the sign of the amount of change is important: if the original amount has increased, the change will be positive; if the original amount has decreased, the change will be negative. In the equations below, the percent is a decimal value that needs to be multiplied by 100 to get the actual percentage:

- $percent\ change = \frac{amount\ of\ chan}{original\ amount}$

- $amount\ of\ change = original\ amount \times percent\ change$

- $original\ amount = \frac{amount\ of\ chan}{percent\ chan}$

> **Did You Know?**
>
> Seeing the following words can indicate that a math problem concerns percent change: *discount, markup, sale, increase, decrease.*

Practice Questions

48. A computer software retailer marks up its games by 40% above the wholesale price when it sells them to customers. Find the price of a game for a customer if the game costs the retailer $25.

49. A golf shop pays its wholesaler $40 for a certain club, and then sells it to a golfer for $75. What is the markup rate?

50. A shoe store charges a 40% markup on the shoes it sells. How much did the store pay for a pair of shoes purchased by a customer for $63?

51. An item originally priced at $55 is marked 25% off. What is the sale price?

52. James wants to put an 18 foot by 51 foot garden in his backyard. If he does, it will reduce the size of his yard by 24%. What will be the area of the remaining yard space?

Comparison of Rational Numbers

Number comparison problems present numbers in different formats and ask the test taker which number is larger or smaller, or whether the numbers are equivalent. An important step in solving these types of problems is to convert the numbers to the same format so that it is easier to compare them. If numbers are given in the same format, or after converting them, determine which number is smaller or if the numbers are equal. Remember that, for negative numbers, higher numbers are actually smaller.

Practice Questions

53. Is $4\frac{3}{4}$ greater than, equal to, or less than $\frac{18}{4}$?

54. Which of the following numbers has the GREATEST value: 104.56, 104.5, or 104.6?

55. Is 65% greater than, less than, or equal to $\frac{13}{20}$?

Exponents and Radicals

Exponents tell us how many times to multiply a base number by itself. In the following example, the base number is 2 and the exponent is 4:

- $2^4 = 2 \times 2 \times 2 \times 2 = 16$

Exponents are also called "**powers**":

- 5 to the third power $= 5^3 = 5 \times 5 \times 5 = 125$.

Some exponents have special names:

- "x to the second power" is also called "x squared," and "x to the third power" is also called "x cubed." The number 3 squared $= 3^2 = 3 \times 3 = 9$.

Radicals are expressions that use roots. They are written in the form $\sqrt[a]{x}$, where $a =$ the **radical power** and $x =$ the **radicand**. The solution to the radical $\sqrt[3]{8}$ is the number that, when multiplied by itself 3 times, equals 8. Therefore, $\sqrt[3]{8} = 2$ because $2 \times 2 \times 2 = 8$.

When the radical power is not written, it is assumed to be 2; therefore $\sqrt{9} = 3$ because $3 \times 3 = 9$.

Radicals can also be written as exponents, where the power is a fraction. For example, $x^{\frac{1}{3}} = \sqrt[3]{x}$.

Additional rules for working with exponents and radicals appear in Table 3.4.

Table 3.4. Exponents and Radicals Rules	
Rule	**Example**
$x^0 = 1$	$5^0 = 1$
$x^1 = x$	$5^1 = 5$
$x^a + x^b = x^{a+b}$	$5^2 + 5^3 = 5^5 = 3,125$
$(xy)^a = x^a y^a$	$(5 \times 6)^2 = 5^2 \times 6^2 = 900$

Table 3.4. Exponents and Radicals Rules

Rule	Example
$(x^a)^b = x^{ab}$	$(5^2)^3 = 5^6 = 15{,}625$
$\dfrac{x^a}{y} = \dfrac{x^a}{y^a}$	$\left(\dfrac{5}{6}\right)^2 = \dfrac{5^2}{6^2} = \dfrac{25}{36}$
$\dfrac{x^a}{x^b} = x^{a-b} \ (x \neq 0)$	$\dfrac{5^4}{5^3} = 5^1 = 5$
$x^{-a} = \dfrac{1}{x^a} \ (x \neq 0)$	$5^{-2} = \dfrac{1}{5^2} = \dfrac{1}{25}$
$x^{\frac{1}{3}} = \sqrt[a]{x}$	$25^{\frac{1}{2}} = \sqrt[2]{25} = 5$
$\sqrt[a]{x \times y} = \sqrt[a]{x} \times \sqrt[a]{y}$	$\sqrt[3]{8 \times 27} = \sqrt[3]{8} \times \sqrt[3]{27} = 2 \times 3 = 6$
$\sqrt[a]{\dfrac{x}{y}} = \dfrac{\sqrt[a]{x}}{\sqrt[a]{y}}$	$\sqrt[3]{\dfrac{27}{8}} = \dfrac{\sqrt[3]{27}}{\sqrt[3]{8}}$
$\sqrt[a]{x^b} = x^{\frac{b}{3}}$	$\sqrt[2]{5^4} = 5^{\frac{4}{2}} = 5^2 = 25$

Practice Questions

56. Simplify the expression $2^4 \times 2^2$

57. Simplify the expression $(3^4)^{-1}$

58. Simplify the expression $\left(\dfrac{9}{4}\right)^{\frac{1}{2}}$

Matrices

A **matrix** is an array of numbers aligned into horizontal rows and vertical columns. It is described by the number of rows (m) and columns (n) that it contains. For example, a matrix with 3 rows and 4 columns is a 3 × 4 matrix, as shown below:

$$\begin{bmatrix} 2 & -3 & 5 & 0 \\ 4 & -6 & 2 & 11 \\ 3.5 & 7 & 2.78 & -1.2 \end{bmatrix}$$

To add or subtract two matrices, simply add or subtract the corresponding numbers in each matrix. Only matrices with the same dimensions can be added or subtracted; the resulting matrix will also have the same dimensions.

In order to multiply two matrices, the number of columns in the first matrix must equal the number of rows in the second matrix. To multiply the matrices, multiply the numbers in each row of the first by the numbers in the column of the second and add. The resulting matrix will have the same number of rows as the first matrix and the same number of columns as the second matrix. Note that the order of the matrices is important when they are being multiplied: *AB* is not the same as *BA*.

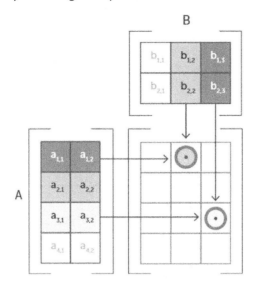

Figure 3.2. Matrix Multiplication

To multiply a matrix by a single number or variable, simply multiply each value within the matrix by that number or variable.

Practice Questions

59. Simplify: $\begin{bmatrix} 6 & 4 & -8 \\ -3 & 1 & 0 \end{bmatrix} + \begin{bmatrix} 5 & -3 & -2 \\ -3 & 4 & 9 \end{bmatrix}$

60. Solve for x and y: $\begin{bmatrix} x & 6 \\ 4 & y \end{bmatrix} + \begin{bmatrix} 3 & 2 \\ 8 & -1 \end{bmatrix} = \begin{bmatrix} 11 & 8 \\ 12 & 4 \end{bmatrix}$

61. If $A = \begin{bmatrix} 1 & 3 & 0 \\ 6 & 2 & 4 \end{bmatrix}$ and $B = \begin{bmatrix} 5 & 3 \\ 2 & 1 \\ 4 & 7 \end{bmatrix}$, what is AB?

62. Simplify: $6x \begin{bmatrix} 2 & -3 \\ 6 & 4 \end{bmatrix}$

Chapter Four

Algebra

Algebraic Expressions

Algebraic expressions and equations include **variables**, or letters that stand in for numbers. These expressions and equations are made up of **terms**, which are groups of numbers and variables (e.g., $2xy$). An **expression** is simply a set of terms (e.g., $\frac{2x}{3yz} + 2$). When those terms are joined only by addition or subtraction, the expression is called a **polynomial** (e.g., $2x + 3yz$). When working with expressions, you will need to use many different mathematical properties and operations, including addition/subtraction, multiplication/division, exponents, roots, distribution, and the order of operations.

To **evaluate an algebraic expression**, simply plug the given value(s) in for the appropriate variable(s) in the expression.

Practice Question

1. Evaluate $2x + 6y - 3z$ if $x = 2$, $y = 4$, and $z = -3$.

Adding and Subtracting Expressions

Only **like terms**, which have the exact same variable(s), can be added or subtracted. **Constants** are numbers without variables attached, and those can be added and subtracted together as well. When simplifying an expression, like terms should be added or subtracted so that no individual group of variables occurs in more than one term. For example, the expression $5x + 6xy$ is in its simplest form, while $5x + 6xy - 11xy$ is not in its simplest form because the term xy appears more than once.

Practice Question

2. Simplify the expression: $5xy + 7y + 2yz + 11xy - 5yz$

Multiplying and Dividing Expressions

To multiply a single term by another, simply multiply the coefficients and then multiply the variables. Remember that the exponents are added together when multiplying variables with exponents. For example:

$$(x^5y)(x^3y^4) = x^8y^5$$

When multiplying a term by a set of terms inside parentheses, each term inside the parentheses needs to be distributed, as shown in Figure 4.1.

When variables occur in both the numerator and denominator of a fraction, they cancel each other out. So, a fraction with variables in its simplest form will not have the same variable on the top and bottom.

$$a(b+c) = ab + ac$$

Figure 4.1. Distribution

Practice Questions

3. Simplify the expression: $(3x^4y^2z)(2y^4z^5)$

4. Simplify the expression: $(2y^2)(y^3 + 2xy^2z + 4z)$

5. Simplify the expression: $(5x + 2)(3x + 3)$

6. Simplify the expression: $\frac{2x^4y^3z}{8x^2z^2}$

Factoring Expressions

Factoring means to split one expression into the multiplication of two expressions. It requires finding the highest common factor and dividing terms by that number. For example, in the expression $15x + 10$, the highest common factor is 5 because both terms are divisible by 5: $\frac{15x}{5} = 3x$ and $\frac{10}{5} = 2$. When you factor the expression you get $5(3x + 2)$.

Sometimes it is difficult to find the highest common factor. In such cases, whether or not the expression fits a polynomial identity must be considered. A **polynomial** is an expression with more than one term. Expressions can be easily factored if the common polynomials listed below are easily recognized:

- $a^2 - b^2 = (a + b)(a - b)$
- $a^2 + 2ab + b^2 = (a + b)(a + b) = (a + b)^2$
- $a^2 - 2ab + b^2 = (a - b)(a - b) = (a - b)^2$
- $a^3 + b^3 = (a + b)(a^2 - ab + b^2)$
- $a^3 - b^3 = (a - b)(a^2 + ab + b^2)$

Practice Questions

7. Factor the expression: $27x^2 - 9x$

8. Factor the expression: $25x^2 - 16$

9. Factor the expression: $100x^2 + 60x + 9$

Linear Equations

An **equation** is a statement that says that two expressions are equal to each other. Equations always include an equal sign (e.g., $3x + 2xy = 17$). A **linear equation** has only two variables, and on a graph, linear equations form a straight line.

Solving Linear Equations

To solve an equation, the terms on each side need to be manipulated in order to isolate the variable; in other words, if you want to find x, you have to get the x alone on one side of the equal sign. To do this, many of the tools discussed above will need to be used: distributing, dividing, adding or subtracting like terms, or finding common denominators.

Think of each side of the equation as the two sides of a seesaw—as long as the two people on each end weigh the same amount (no matter what that amount is), the seesaw will be balanced:

- If there is a 120-pound person on each end, the seesaw is balanced.

- Giving each person a 10-pound rock to hold will change the weight on each end, but the seesaw itself will stay balanced.

  - Equations work the same way: people can add, subtract, multiply, or divide whatever they want, as long as they do the same thing to both sides.

Most equations that will be encountered on the SAT can be solved using the same basic steps:

1. Distribute to get rid of parentheses.

2. Use LCD to get rid of fractions.

3. Add/subtract like terms on either side.

4. Add/subtract so that constants appear on only one side of the equation.

5. Multiply/divide to isolate the variable.

> **Helpful Hint**:
>
> If you are stumped on a multiple-choice question, try plugging the answer options back into the original problem to see which one works.

Practice Questions

10. Solve for x: $25x + 12 = 62$

11. Solve the following equation for x: $2x - 4(2x + 3) = 24$

12. Solve the following equation for x: $\frac{x}{3} + \frac{1}{2} = \frac{x}{6} - \frac{5}{12}$

13. Find the value of x: $2(x + y) - 7x = 14x + 3$

Graphing Linear Equations

Linear equations can be plotted as straight lines on a coordinate plane. The **x-axis** is always the horizontal axis and the **y-axis** is always the vertical axis. The x-axis is positive to the right of the y-axis and negative to the left. The y-axis is positive above the x-axis and negative below it. To describe the location of any point on the graph, write the coordinates in the form (x, y). The origin, the point where the x- and y-axes cross, is $(0,0)$.

The **y-intercept** is the y coordinate where the line crosses the y-axis. The **slope** is a measure of how steep the line is. Slope is calculated by dividing the change along the y-axis by the change along the x-axis between any two points on the line.

Linear equations are easiest to graph when they are written in **point-slope form**: $y = mx + b$. The constant m represents slope and the constant b represents the y-intercept. Knowing two points along the line (x_1, y_1) and (x_2, y_2) can help you calculate the slope by using the following equation:

- $m = \frac{y_2 - y_1}{x_2 - x_1}$

If you know the slope and one other point along the line, you can calculate the y-intercept by plugging the number 0 in for x_2 and solving for y_2.

When graphing a linear equation, first plot the y-intercept. Next, plug in values for x to solve for y and then plot additional points. Connect the points with a straight line.

Practice Questions

14. Find the slope of the line: $\frac{3y}{2} + 3 = x$

15. Plot the linear equation: $2y - 4x = 6$

Systems of Equations

A **system of equations** is a group of related questions that share the same variable. Questions on the SAT will most likely involve two equations that each have two variables, although you may also solve sets of equations with any number of variables as long as there are a corresponding number of equations. For example, to solve a system with four variables, you need four equations.

There are two main methods used to solve systems of equations:

- In **substitution**, solve one equation for a single variable, and then substitute the solution for that variable into the second equation to solve for the other variable.

- **Elimination** can also be used by adding equations together to cancel variables and solve for one of them.

Practice Questions

16. Solve the following system of equations: $3y - 4 + x = 0$ and $5x + 6y = 11$

17. Solve the system: $2x + 4y = 8$ and $4x + 2y = 10$

Building Equations

Word problems describe a situation or a problem without explicitly providing an equation to solve. It is therefore up to the test taker to build an algebraic equation in order to solve the problem. This can be done using the following steps:

- Translate the words into mathematical operations.

- Represent the unknown quantity with a variable.

  o If there is more than one unknown, more than one equation will likely be needed.

  o Solve the system of equations by substituting expressions. (Remember to keep the variables straight.)

Practice Questions

18. David, Jesse, and Mark shoveled snow during their snow day and made a total of $100. They agreed to split it based on how much each person worked. David will take $10 more than Jesse, who will take $15 more than Mark. How much money will David get?

19. The sum of three consecutive numbers is 54. What is the MIDDLE number?

20. There are 42 people on the varsity football team. This is 8 more than half the number of people on the swim team. There are 6 fewer boys on the swim team than girls. How many girls are on the swim team?

Linear Inequalities

Inequalities look like equations, except that instead of having an equal sign, they have one of the following symbols:

- greater than: the expression left of the symbol is larger than the expression on the right
- $<$ less than: the expression left of the symbol is smaller than the expression on the right
- $\geq$ greater than or equal to: the expression left of the symbol is larger than or equal to the expression on the right
- $\leq$ less than or equal to: the expression left of the symbol is less than or equal to the expression on the right

Inequalities are solved like linear and algebraic equations. The only difference is that the symbol must be reversed when both sides of the equation are multiplied by a negative number.

Graphing a linear inequality is just like graphing a linear equation, except that you shade the area on one side of the line. The following steps can be used to graph a linear inequality:

1. Rearrange the inequality expression into $y = mx + b$ form.
2. Next, treat the inequality symbol like an equal sign and plot the line.
3. If the inequality symbol is < or >, make a broken line.
   a. If the symbol is $\leq$ or $\geq$, make a solid line.
4. Finally, shade the correct side of the graph:
   a. For $y < mx + b$ or $y \leq mx + b$, shade below the line.
   b. For $y > mx + b$ or $y \geq mx + b$, shade above the line.

Practice Questions

21. Solve for x: $-7x + 2 < 6 - 5x$

22. Plot the inequality: $-3 \geq 4 - y$

Quadratic Equations

A **quadratic equation** is any equation in the form $ax^2 + bx + c = 0$. In quadratic equations, x is the variable and a, b, and c are all known numbers; a can never be 0.

Solving Quadratic Equations

There is more than one way to solve a quadratic equation. One way is by **factoring**. By rearranging the expression $ax^2 + bx + c$ into one factor multiplied by another factor, you can easily solve for the roots, the values of x for which the quadratic expression equals 0. Another way to solve a quadratic equation is by using the quadratic formula:

$$\frac{-b \pm \sqrt{b^2 - 4ac}}{2^a}$$

The expression $b^2 - 4ac$ is called the **discriminant**; when it is positive you will get two real numbers for x, and when it is negative you will get one real number and one imaginary number for x. When the discriminant is zero, you will get one real number for x.

Practice Questions

23. Factor the quadratic equation $-2x^2 = 14x$ and find the roots.

24. Use the quadratic formula to solve for x: $3x^2 = 7x - 2$.

Graphing Quadratic Equations

Graphing a quadratic equation forms a parabola. A **parabola** is a symmetrical, horseshoe shaped curve; a **vertical axis** passes through its vertex. Each term in the equation $ax^2 + bx + c = 0$ affects the shape of the parabola. A bigger value for a makes the curve narrower, while a smaller value makes the curve wider. A negative value for a flips the parabola upside down. The **axis of symmetry** is the vertical line $x = \frac{-b}{2a}$.

To find the y coordinate for the vertex (the highest or lowest point on the parabola), plug this value for x into the expression $ax^2 + bx + c$. The easiest way to graph a quadratic equation is to find the axis of symmetry, solve for the vertex, and then create a table of points by plugging in other numbers for x and solving for y. Plot these points and trace the parabola.

Practice Question

25. Graph the equation: $x^2 + 4x + 1 = 0$

Functions

Functions describe how an input relates to an output. Linear equations, sine, and cosine are examples of functions. In a function, there must be <u>one and only one</u> output for each input. For example, $\sqrt{x}$ is not a function because there are two outputs for any one input: $\sqrt{4} = 2, -2$.

Describing Functions

Functions are often written in $f(x)$ form:

- $f(x) = x^2$ means that for input x the output is x^2. In relating functions to linear equations, you can think of $f(x)$ as equivalent to y.

The **domain** of a function is all the possible inputs of that function. The **range** of a function includes the outputs of the inputs. For example, for the function $f(x) = x^2$, if the domain includes all positive and negative integers, then the range will include 0 and only positive integers. When you graph a function, the domain is plotted on the x-axis and the range is plotted on the y-axis.

Practice Questions

26. Given $f(x) = 2x - 10$, find $f(9)$.

27. Given $f(x) = \frac{4}{x}$ with a domain of all positive integers except zero, and $g(x) = \frac{4}{x}$ with a domain of all positive and negative integers except zero, which function has a range that includes the number -2?

Exponential Functions

An **exponential function** is in the form $f(x) = a^x$, where $a > 0$. When $a > 1$, $f(x)$ approaches infinity as x increases and approaches 0 (zero) as x decreases. When $0 < a < 1$, $f(x)$ approaches 0 (zero) as x increases and infinity as x increases. When $a = 1$, $f(x) = 1$. The graph of an exponential function where $a \neq 1$ will have a horizontal asymptote along the x-axis; the graph will never cross below the x-axis. The graph of an exponential function where $a = 1$ will be a horizontal line at $y = 1$. All graphs of exponential functions include the points $(0, 1)$ and $(1, a)$.

Practice Questions

28. Graph the function: $f(x) = 3^x$.

29. Given $f(x) = 2^x$, solve for x when $f(x) = 64$.

Logarithmic Functions

A **logarithmic function** is the inverse of an exponential function. The definition of a log is if $\log_a x = b$, then $a^b = x$. Logarithmic functions are written in the form $f(x) = \log_a x$, where a is any number greater than 0, except for 1. If a is not shown, it is assumed that $a = 10$. The function $ln\ x$ is called a **natural log** and is equal to $\log_e x$. When $0 < a < 1$, $f(x)$ approaches infinity as x approaches zero and it approaches negative infinity as x increases. When $a > 1$, $f(x)$ approaches negative infinity as x approaches zero and infinity as x increases. In either case, the graph of a logarithmic function has a vertical asymptote along the y-axis; the graph will never cross to the left of the y-axis. All graphs of logarithmic functions include the points $(1, 0)$ and $(a, 1)$.

Practice Questions

30. Graph the function $f(x) = \log 4x$.

31. Given $f(x) = \log_1 3x$, solve for $f(81)$.

Arithmetic and Geometric Sequences

Sequences are patterns of numbers. In most questions about sequences you must determine the pattern. In an **arithmetic sequence**, add or subtract the same number between terms. In a **geometric sequence**, multiply or divide by the same number between terms. For example, 2, 6, 10, 14, 18 and 11, 4, −3, −10, −17 are arithmetic sequences because you add 4 to each term in the first example and you subtract 7 from each term in the second example. The sequence 5, 15, 45, 135 is a geometric sequence because you multiply each term by 3. In arithmetic sequences, the number by which you add or subtract is called the **common difference**. In geometric sequences, the number by which you multiply or divide is called the **common ratio**. In an arithmetic sequence, the nth term (a_n) can be found by calculating $a_n = a_1 + (n − 1)d$, where d is the common difference and a_1 is the first term in the sequence. In a geometric sequence, $a_n = a_1(r^n)$, where r is the common ratio.

Practice Questions

32. Find the common difference and the next term of the following sequence: 5, −1, −7, −13.

33. Find the twelfth term of the following sequence: 2, 6, 18, 54.

34. The fourth term of a sequence is 9. The common difference is 11. What is the tenth term?

Absolute Value

The **absolute value** of a number (represented by the symbol | |) is its distance from zero, not its value. For example, $|3| = 3$, and $|−3| = 3$ because both 3 and −3 are three units from zero. The absolute value of a number is always positive.

Equations with absolute values will have two answers, so you need to set up two equations. The first is simply the equation with the absolute value symbol removed. For the second equation, isolate the absolute value on one side of the equation and multiply the other side of the equation by −1.

Practice Questions

35. Solve for x: $|2x − 3| = x + 1$

36. Solve for y: $2|y + 4| = 10$

Solving Word Problems

Any of the math concepts discussed here can be turned into a word problem, and you will likely see word problems in various formats throughout the test. (In fact, you may have noticed that several examples in the ratio and proportion sections were word problems.) Be sure to read the entire problem before beginning to solve it: a common mistake is to provide an answer to a question that wasn't actually asked. Also, remember that not all of the information provided in a problem is necessarily needed to solve it.

When working multiple-choice word problems like those on the SAT, it's important to check your work. Many of the incorrect answer options will be answers that result from common mistakes. So even if a

solution you calculated is listed as an answer option, it does not necessarily mean that you have done the problem correctly—you have to check your own answer to be sure.

The following list describes some general steps for word-problem solving:

1. Read the entire problem and determine what the question is asking.

2. List all of the given data and define the variables.

3. Determine the formula(s) needed or set up equations from the information in the problem.

4. Solve.

5. Check your answer. (Is the amount too large or small? Is the answer in the correct unit of measure?)

Word problems generally contain key words that can help you determine which math processes may be required in order to solve them.

- **Addition:** *added, combined, increased by, in all, total, perimeter, sum,* and *more than*

- **Subtraction:** *how much more, less than, fewer than, exceeds, difference,* and *decreased*

- **Multiplication:** *of, times, area,* and *product*

- **Division:** *distribute, share, average, per, out of, percent,* and *quotient*

- **Equals:** *is, was, are, amounts to,* and *were*

Basic Word Problems

A **word problem** in algebra is just an equation or a set of equations described using words. Your task when solving these problems is to turn the story of the problem into mathematical equations. Converting units can often help you avoid operations with fractions when dealing with time.

Practice Questions

37. A store owner bought a case of 48 backpacks for $476.00. He sold 17 of the backpacks in his store for $18 each, and the rest were sold to a school for $15 each. What was the store owner's profit?

38. Thirty students in Mr. Joyce's room are working on projects over 2 days. The first day, he gave them $\frac{3}{5}$ of an hour to work. On the second day, he gave them $\frac{1}{2}$ as much time as the first day. How much time did each student have to work on the project?

Distance Word Problems

Distance word problems involve something traveling at a constant or average speed. Whenever you read a problem that involves how fast, how far, or for how long, you should think of the distance equation, where d stands for *distance*, r for *rate (speed)*, and t for time.

These problems can be solved by setting up a grid with d, r, and t along the top and each moving object on the left. When setting up the grid, make sure the units are consistent. For example, if the distance is in meters and the time is in seconds, the rate should be meters per second.

Practice Questions

39. Will drove from his home to the airport at an average speed of 30 mph. He then boarded a helicopter and flew to the hospital at an average speed of 60 mph. The entire distance was 150 miles, and the trip took 3 hours. Find the distance from the airport to the hospital.

40. Two riders on horseback start at the same time from opposite ends of a field that is 45 miles long. One horse is moving at 14 mph and the second horse is moving at 16 mph. How long after they begin will they meet?

Work Problems

Work problems involve situations where several people or machines are doing work at different rates. Your task is usually to figure out how long it will take these people or machines to complete a task while working together. The trick to doing work problems is to figure out how much of the project each person or machine completes in the same unit of time.

> **Did You Know?**
>
> The SAT will give you most formulas you need to solve problems, but they won't give you the formulas for percent change or work problems.

For example, you might calculate how much of a wall a person can paint in 1 hour, or how many boxes an assembly line can pack in 1 minute. The next step is to set up an equation to solve for the total time. This equation is usually similar to the equation for distance, but here $work = rate \times time$.

Practice Questions

41. Bridget can clean an entire house in 12 hours while it takes her brother Tom 8 hours to do the same. How long would it take for Bridget and Tom to clean 2 houses together?

42. Farmer Dan needs to water his cornfield. One hose can water a field 1.25 times faster than a second hose. When both hoses are running, they water the field together in 5 hours. How long would it take to water the field if only the slower hose is used?

43. Ben takes 2 hours to pick 500 apples, and Frank takes 3 hours to pick 450 apples. How long will they take, working together, to pick 1000 apples?

Chapter Five

Geometry

Area and Perimeter

area and perimeter problems require you to use the equations shown in the table below to find either the area inside a shape or the distance around it (the perimeter). These equations will not be given on the test, so you need to have them memorized on test day.

Table 5.1. Area and Perimeter Equations		
Shape	**Area**	**Perimeter**
Circle	$A = \pi r2$	$C = 2\pi r = d$
Triangle	$A = b \times h2$	$P = s1 + s2 + s3$
Square	$A = s2$	$P = 4s$
Rectangle	$A = l \times w$	$P = 2l + 2w$

Practice Questions

1. A farmer has purchased 100 meters of fencing to enclose his rectangular garden. If one side of the garden is 20 meters long and the other is 28 meters long, how much fencing will the farmer have left over?

2. Taylor is going to paint a square wall that is 3.5 meters high. How much paint will he need?

Volume

Volume is the amount of space taken up by a three-dimensional object. Different formulas are used to find the volumes of different shapes.

Table 5.2. Volume Formulas	
Shape	**Volume**
cylinder	$V = \pi r2h$
pyramid	$V = l \times w \times h/$
cone	$V = \dfrac{\pi r^2 h}{3}$
sphere	$V = \dfrac{4}{3}\pi r3$

Practice Questions

3. Charlotte wants to fill her circular swimming pool with water. The pool has a diameter of 6 meters and is 1 meter deep. How many cubic meters of water will she need to fill the pool?

4. Danny has a fishbowl that is filled to the brim with water. He purchased some spherical glass marbles to line the bottom of it. He dropped in four marbles and water spilled out of the fishbowl. If the radius of each marble is 1 centimeter, how much water spilled?

Circles

The definition of a circle is the set of points that are equal distance from a center point. The distance from the center to any given point on the circle is the radius. If you draw a straight line segment across the circle going through the center, the distance along the line segment from one side of the circle to the other is called the diameter. The radius is always equal to half the diameter: $d = 2r$.

A central angle is formed by drawing radii out from the center to two points A and B along the circle. The intercepted arc is the portion of the circle (the arc length) between points A and B. You can find the intercepted arc length l if you know the central angle θ and vice versa:

$$l = 2\pi r \frac{\theta}{360}°$$

A chord is a line segment that connects two points on a circle. Unlike the diameter, a chord does not have to go through the center. You can find the chord length if you know either the central angle θ or the radius of the circle r and the distance from the center of the circle to the chord d (d must be at a right angle to the chord):

- If you know the central angle, chord $length = 2r \sin \theta$
- If you know the radius and distance, chord $length = 2 \sqrt{r 2 - d2}$

A secant is similar to a chord; it connects two points on a circle. The difference is that a secant is a line, not a line segment, so it extends outside of the circle on either side.

A tangent is a straight line that touches a circle at only one point.

A sector is the area within a circle that is enclosed by a central angle; if a circle is a pie, a sector is the piece of pie cut by two radii. You can find the area of a sector if you know either the central angle θ or the arc length s.

If you know the central angle, the area of the sector $= \pi r 2 \theta$

If you know the arc length, the area of a sector $= 1 rl$

There are two other types of angles you can create in or around a circle. inscribed angles are inside the circle: the vertex is a point P on the circle and the rays extend to two other points on the circle (A and B). As long as A and B remain constant, you can move the vertex P anywhere along the circle and the inscribed angle will be the same. circumscribed angles are outside of the circle: the rays are formed by two tangent lines that touch the circle at points A and B.

You can find the inscribed angle if you know the radius of the circle r and the arc length l between A and B:

$$Inscribed\ angle = \frac{90°}{\pi r}$$

To find the circumscribed angle, find the central angle formed by the same points A and B and subtract that angle from 180°.

Practice Questions

5. A circle has a diameter of 10 centimeters. What is the intercepted arc length between points A and B if the central angle between those points measures 46°?

6. A chord is formed by line segment QP. The radius of the circle is 5 cm and the chord length is 6 cm. Find the distance from center C to the chord.

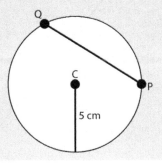

Congruence

congruence means having the same size and shape. Two shapes are congruent if you can turn (rotate), flip (reflect), and/or slide (translate) one to fit perfectly on top of the other. Two angles are congruent if they measure the same number of degrees; they do not have to face the same direction nor must they necessarily have rays of equal length. If two triangles have one of the combinations of congruent sides and/or angles listed below, then those triangles are congruent:

- sss – side, side, side
- asa – angle, side, angle
- sas – side, angle, side
- aas – angle, angle, side

There are a number of common sets of congruent angles in geometry. An isosceles triangle has two sides of equal length (called the legs) and two congruent angles. If you bisect an isosceles triangle by drawing a line perpendicular to the third side (called the base), you will form two congruent right triangles.

Where two lines cross and form an X, the opposite angles are congruent and are called vertical angles. parallel lines are lines that never cross; if you cut two parallel lines by a transversal, you will form four pairs of congruent corresponding angles.

A parallelogram is a quadrilateral in which both pairs of opposite sides are parallel and congruent (of equal length). In a parallelogram, the two pairs of opposite angles are also congruent. If you divide a parallelogram by either of the diagonals, you will form two congruent triangles.

Practice Questions

7. Kate and Emily set out for a bike ride together from their house. They ride 6 miles north, then Kate turns 30° to the west and Emily turns 30° to the east. They both ride another 8 miles. If Kate rides 12 miles to return home, how far must Emily ride to get home?

8. Angle *A* measure 53°. Find angle *H*

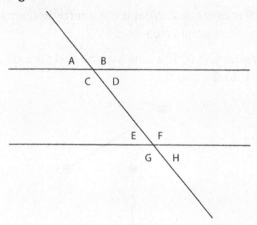

Pythagorean Theorem

Shapes with 3 sides are known as triangles. In addition to knowing the formulas for their area and perimeter, you should also know the Pythagorean Theorem, which describes the relationship between the three sides (a, b, and c) of a triangle:

$$a^2 + b^2 = c^2$$

Practice Question

9. Erica is going to run a race in which she'll run 3 miles due north and 4 miles due east. She'll then run back to the starting line. How far will she run during this race?

Trigonometry

Using trigonometry, you can calculate an angle in a right triangle based on the ratio of two sides of that triangle. You can also calculate one of the side lengths using the measure of an angle and another side. sine (sin), cosine (cos), and tangent (tan) corre- spond to the three possible ratios of side lengths. They are defined below:

$$\sin \theta = \frac{opposite}{hypotenus} \quad \cos \theta = \frac{adjacent}{hypotenus} \quad tap\, \theta = \frac{opposite}{adjacent}$$

Opposite is the side opposite from the angle θ, adjacent is the side adjacent to the angle θ, and hypotenuse is the longest side of the triangle, opposite from the right angle. SOH- CAH-TOA is an acronym to help you remember which ratio goes with which function.

When solving for a side or an angle in a right triangle, first identify which function to use based on the known lengths or angle.

Practice Questions

10. Phil is hanging holiday lights. To do so safely, he must lean his 20-foot ladder against the outside of his house at an angle of 15° or less. How far from the house can he safely place the base of the ladder?

11. Grace is practicing shooting hoops. She is 5 feet 4 inches tall. Her basketball hoop is 10 feet tall. From 8 feet away, at what angle does she have to look up to see the hoop? Assume that her eyes are 4 inches lower than that top of her head.

Coordinate Geometry

Coordinate geometry is the study of points, lines, and shapes that have been graphed on a set of axes.

Points, Lines, and Planes

In coordinate geometry, points are plotted on a coordinate plane, a two-dimensional plane in which the x-axis indicates horizontal direction and the y-axis indicates vertical direction. The intersection of these two axes is the origin. Points are defined by their location in relation to the horizontal and vertical axes. The coordinates of a point are written (x, y). The coordinates of the origin are (0, 0). The x-coordinates to the right of the origin and the y-coordinates above it are positive; the x-coordinates to the left of the origin and the y-coordinates below it are negative.

A line is formed by connecting any two points on a coordinate plane; lines are con- tinuous in both directions. Lines can be defined by their slope, or steepness, and their y-intercept, or the point at which they intersect the y-axis. A line is represented by the equation y = mx + b. The constant m represents slope and the constant b represents the y-intercept.

Practice Questions

12. Matt parks his car near a forest where he goes hiking. From his car, he hikes 1 mile north, 2 miles east, then 3 miles west. If his car represents the origin, find the coordinates of Matt's current location.

13. A square is drawn on a coordinate plane. The bottom corners are located at $(-2,3)$ and $(4,3)$. What are the coordinates for the top right corner?

Distance and Midpoint Formulas

To determine the distance between the points (x1, y1) and (x2, y2) from a grid use the formula:

$$d = \sqrt{(x_2 - x_1)^2 + (y_2 - y_1)^2}$$

The midpoint, which is halfway between the 2 points, is the point:

$$m = \frac{x_1 + x_2}{2}, \frac{y_1 + y_2}{2}$$

Practice Questions

14. What is the distance between points $(3, -6)$ and $(-5,2)$?

15. What is the midpoint between points $(3, -6)$ and $(-5,2)$?

Chapter Six

Statistics and Probability

Describing Sets of Data

statistics is the study of sets of data. The goal of statistics is to take a group of values— numerical answers from a survey, for example—and look for patterns in how that data is distributed.

When looking at a set of data, it's helpful to consider the measures of central tendency, a group of values that describe the central or typical data point from the set. The SAT covers three measures of central tendency: mean, median, and mode.

mean is the mathematical term for average. To find the mean, total all the terms and divide by the number of terms. The median is the middle number of a given set. To find the median, put the terms in numerical order; the middle number will be the median. In the case of a set of even numbers, the middle two numbers are averaged. mode is the number which occurs most frequently within a given set. If two different numbers both appear with the highest frequency, they are both the mode.

When examining a data set, also consider measures of variability, which describe how the data is dispersed around the central data point. The SAT covers two measures of variability: range and standard deviation. range is simply the difference between the largest and smallest values in the set. standard deviation is a measure of how dispersed the data is, or how far it reaches from the mean.

Practice Questions

1. Find the mean of 24, 27, and 18.

2. The mean of three numbers is 45. If two of the numbers are 38 and 43, what is the third number?

3. What is the median of 24, 27, and 18?

4. What is the median of 24, 27, 18, and 19?

5. What is the mode of 2, 5, 4, 4, 3, 2, 8, 9, 2, 7, 2, and 2?

6. What is the standard deviation of 62, 63, 61, and 66?

Graphs and Charts

These questions require you to interpret information from graphs and charts; they are pretty straightforward as long as you pay careful attention to detail. There are several different graph and chart types that may appear on the SAT.

Bar Graphs

Bar graphs present the numbers of an item that exist in different categories. The categories are shown on the x-axis, and the number of items are shown on the y-axis. Bar graphs are usually used to easily compare amounts.

Pie Charts

pie charts present parts of a whole, and are often used with percentages. Together, all the slices of the pie add up to the total number of items, or 100%.

Line Graphs

Line graphs show trends over time. The number of each item represented by the graph will be on the y-axis, and time will be on the x-axis.

Histograms

A histogram shows a distribution of types within a whole in bar chart form. While they look like bar graphs, they are more similar to pie charts: they show you parts of a whole.

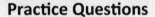

Practice Questions

7. The chart below shows rainfall in inches per month. Which month had the least amount of rainfall? Which had the most?

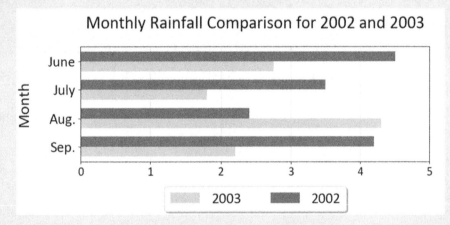

8. Using the chart below, how many more ice cream cones were sold in July than in September?

9. The pie chart below shows the distribution of birthdays in a class of students. How many students have birthdays in the spring or summer?

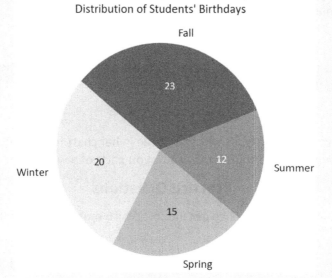

Distribution of Students' Birthdays

10. Using the same graph above, what percentage of students have birthdays in winter?

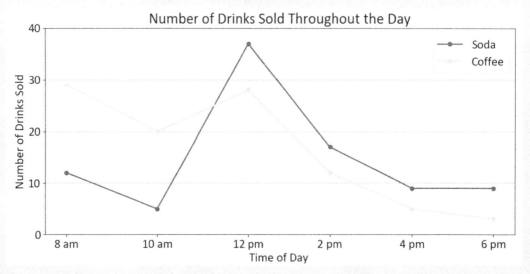

11. The line graph above shows beverage sales at an airport shop throughout the day. Which beverage sold more at 4:00 p.m.?

12. At what time of day were the most beverages sold?

13. The following chart shows the number of cars that traveled through a toll plaza throughout the day. How many cars passed through the toll plaza between 8:00 a.m. and 5:00 p.m.?

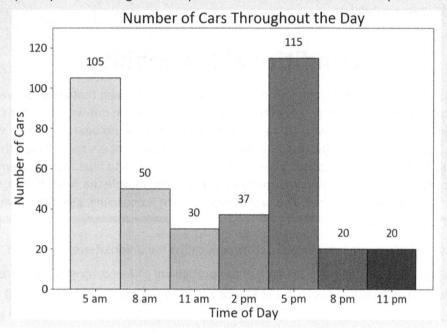

Probability

Probability is the likelihood that an event will take place. This likelihood is expressed as a value between 0 and 1. The closer the probability is to zero, the less likely the event is to occur; the closer the probability is to 1, the more likely it is to occur.

Probability of a Single Event

The probability of an outcome occurring is found by dividing the number of desired outcomes by the number of total possible outcomes. As with percentages, a probability is the ratio of a part to a whole, with the whole being the total number of possibilities, and the part being the number of desired results. Probabilities can be written using percentages (40%), decimals (0.4), fractions, or in words (the probability of an outcome is 2 in 5).

$$probability = \frac{desired\ outcomes}{total\ possible\ outcomes}$$

Practice Questions

14. A bag holds 3 blue marbles, 5 green marbles, and 7 red marbles. If you pick one marble form the bag, what is the probability it will be blue?

15. A bag contains 75 balls. If the probability is 0.6 that a ball selected from the bag will be red, how many red balls are in the bag?

16. A theater has 230 seats: 75 seats are in the orchestra are, 100 seats are in the mezzanine, and 55 seats are in the balcony. If a ticket is selected at random, what is the probability that it will be for either a mezzanine or balcony seat?

17. The probability of selecting a student whose name begins with the letter *S* from a school attendance log is 7%. If there are 42 students whose names begin with *S* enrolled at the school, how many students in total attend it?

Conditional Probability

conditional probability refers to the chances of one event occurring, given that another event has already occurred. independent events are events that have no effect on one another. The classic example is flipping a coin: whether you flip heads or tails one time has no bearing on how you might flip the next time. Your chance of flipping heads is always 50/50. dependent events, on the other hand, have an effect on the next event's probability. If you have a bag full of red and blue marbles, removing a red marble the first time will decrease the probability of picking a red marble the second time, since now there are fewer red marbles in the bag. The probability of event B occurring, given that event A has occurred, is written P(B|A).

The probability of either event A or event B occurring is called the union of events A and B, written A ∪ B. The probability of A ∪ B is equal to the sum of the probability of A occurring and the probability of B occurring, minus the probability of both A and B occurring. The probability of both A and B occurring is called the intersection of events A and B, written A ∩ B. The probability of A ∩ B is equal to the product of the probability of A and the probability of B, given A. Review the equations for the probabilities of unions and intersections below:

$$P(A \cup B) = P(A) + P(B) - P(A \cap B)$$
$$P(A \cap B) = P(A) \times P(B|A)$$

The complement of an event is when the event does not occur. The probability of the complement of event A, written P(A'), is equal to 1 – P(A).

Practice Questions

18. A bad contains 5 red marbles and 11 blue marbles. What is the probability of pulling out a blue marble, followed by a red marble?

19. Caroline randomly draws a playing card from a full deck. What is the chance she will select either a queen or a diamond?

Conditional Probability

Part II Answer Key

Chapter 3

1. $\sqrt{5}$ is an irrational number because it cannot be written as a fraction of two integers. It is a decimal that goes on forever without repeating.

2. $-\sqrt{64}$ can be rewritten as the negative whole number −8, so it is an integer.

3. Subtract the real and imaginary numbers separately:

$$3 - 1 = 2$$
$$5i - (-2i) = 5i + 2i = 7i$$

4. $(-) \times (+) = (-)$

$$-10 \times 47 = -470$$

5. $(-) + (-) = (-)$

$$-65 + -32 = -97$$

6. $(-) \times (+) = (-)$

$-7 \times 4 = -28$, which is less than −7

7. $(-) \div (+) = (-)$

$$-16 \div 2.5 = -6.4$$

8. Use PEMDAS. First, complete operations within parentheses:

$$-(2)^2 - (11)$$

Second, calculate the value of exponential numbers:

$$-(4) - (11)$$

Finally, do addition and subtraction:

$$-4 - 11 = -15$$

9. First, calculate the value of exponential numbers:

$$(25) \div 5 + 4 \times 2$$

Second, calculate division and multiplication from left to right:

$$5 + 8$$

Finally, do addition and subtraction:

$$5 + 8 = 13$$

10. First, complete operations within parentheses:

$$15 \times (12) - 3^3$$

Second, calculate the value of the exponential numbers:

$$15 \times (12) - 27$$

Third, calculate division and multiplication from left to right:

$$180 - 27$$

Finally, do addition and subtraction from left to right

$$180 - 27 = 153$$

11. First, complete operations within parentheses:

$$(10) + 23 - 4^2$$

Second, calculate the value of the exponential numbers:

$$(10) + 23 - 16$$

Finally, do addition and subtraction from left to right:

$$(10) + 23 - 16$$
$$33 - 16 = 17$$

12. 1 yd. = 3 ft.

$$\frac{15}{3} = 5 \text{ yd.}$$

13. 1 gal. = 16 cups

$$\frac{24}{16} = 1.5 \text{ gal.}$$

14. 12 in. = 1 ft.

$$\frac{144}{12} = 12 \text{ ft.}$$

$$12 \text{ ft.} \times 3 \text{ spools} = 36 \text{ ft. of wire}$$

15. This problem can be worked in two steps: finding how many inches are covered in 1 minute, and then converting that value to feet. It can also be worked the opposite way, by finding how many feet the ball travels in 1 second and then converting that to feet traveled per minute. The first method is shown below:

$$1 \text{ min.} = 60 \text{ sec.}$$

$$\frac{6 \text{ in.}}{\text{sec.}} \times 60 \text{ s} = 360 \text{ in.}$$

$$1 \text{ ft.} = 12 \text{ in.}$$

$$\frac{360 \text{ in.}}{12 \text{ in.}} = 30 \text{ ft.}$$

16. $1 \text{ meter} = 1000 \text{ mm}$

$$0.5 \text{ meters} = 500 \text{ mm}$$

17. $1 \text{ kg} = 1000 \text{ g}$

$$\frac{38 \text{ g}}{1000 \text{ g}} = 0.038 \text{ kg}$$

18. $1 \text{ L} = 1000 \text{ cm}^3$

$$10 \text{ L} = 1000 \text{ cm}^3 \times 10$$

$$10 \text{ L} = 10{,}000 \text{ cm}^3$$

19. $1 \text{ cm} = 10 \text{ mm}$

$$10 \text{ cm} - 9.6 \text{ cm} = 0.4 \text{ cm lost}$$

$$0.4 \text{ cm} = 10 \text{ mm} \times 0.4 = 4 \text{ mm were lost}$$

20. $17.07 + 2.52 = 19.59$

21. $7.4 - 6.8 = 0.6 \text{ gal.}$

22. $25 \times 14 = 350$

There are 2 digits after the decimal in 0.25 and one digit after the decimal in 1.4. Therefore the product should have 3 digits after the decimal: 0.350 is the correct answer.

23. Change 0.2 to 2 by moving the decimal one space to the right. Next, move the decimal one space to the right on the dividend; 0.8 will become 8. Now, divide 8 by 2:

$$8 \div 2 = 4$$

24. First, change the divisor to a whole number: 0.25 becomes 25. Next, change the dividend to match the divisor by moving the decimal two spaces to the right, so 40 becomes 4000. Now divide:

$$4000 \div 25 = 160$$

25. 121 and 77 share a common factor of 11. So, if we divide each by 11 we can simplify the fraction:

$$\frac{121}{77} = \frac{11}{11} \times \frac{11}{7} = \frac{11}{7}$$

---

26. Start by dividing the numerator by the denominator: $37 \div 5 = 7$ with a remainder of 2. Now build a mixed number with the whole number and the new numerator:

$$\frac{37}{5} = 7\frac{2}{5}$$

27. For a fraction division problem, invert the second fraction and then multiply and reduce:

$$\frac{7}{8} \div \frac{1}{4} = \frac{7}{8} \times \frac{4}{1} = \frac{28}{8} = \frac{7}{2}$$

28. This is a fraction multiplication problem, so simply multiply the numerators together and the denominators together and then reduce:

$$\frac{1}{12} \times \frac{6}{8} = \frac{6}{96} = \frac{1}{16}$$

Sometimes, if it is possible to do so, it is easier to reduce fractions before multiplying:

$$\frac{1}{12} \times \frac{6}{8} = \frac{1}{12} \times \frac{3}{4} = \frac{3}{48} = \frac{1}{16}$$

29. This is a fraction division problem, so the first step is to convert the mixed number to an improper fraction:

$$1\frac{1}{5} = \frac{5 \times 1}{5} = \frac{1}{5} = \frac{6}{5}$$

Now, divide the fractions. Remember to invert the second fraction, and then multiply normally:

$$\frac{2}{5} \div \frac{6}{5} = \frac{2}{5} \times \frac{5}{6} = \frac{10}{30} = \frac{1}{3}$$

30. This is a fraction multiplication problem:

$$\frac{1}{4} \times 8\frac{1}{2}$$

First, we need to convert the mixed number into an improper fraction:

$$8\frac{1}{2} = \frac{8 \times 2}{2} + \frac{1}{2} = \frac{17}{2}$$

Now, multiply the fractions across the numerators and denominators, and then reduce:

$$\frac{1}{4} \times \frac{81}{2} = \frac{1}{4} \times \frac{17}{2} = \frac{17}{8} \text{ cups of sugar}$$

31. First, multiply each fraction by a factor of 1 to get a common denominator. How do you know which factor of 1 to use? Look at the other fraction and use the number found in that denominator:

$$\frac{2}{3} - \frac{1}{5} = \frac{2}{3}\left(\frac{5}{5}\right) - \frac{1}{5}\left(\frac{3}{3}\right) = \frac{10}{15} - \frac{3}{15}$$

Once the fractions have a common denominator, simply subtract the numerators:

$$\frac{10}{15} - \frac{3}{15} = \frac{7}{15}$$

32. This is a fraction subtraction problem with a mixed number, so the first step is to convert the mixed number to an improper fraction:

$$2\frac{1}{3} = \frac{2 \times 3}{3} + \frac{1}{3} = \frac{7}{3}$$

Next, convert each fraction so they share a common denominator:

$$\frac{7}{3} \times \frac{2}{2} = \frac{14}{6}$$

$$\frac{3}{2} \times \frac{3}{3} = \frac{9}{6}$$

Now, subtract the fractions by subtracting the numerators:

$$\frac{14}{6} - \frac{9}{6} = \frac{5}{6}$$

33. For this fraction addition problem, we need to find a common denominator. Notice that 2 and 4 are both factors of 16, so 16 can be the common denominator:

$$\frac{1}{2} \times \frac{8}{8} = \frac{8}{16}$$

$$\frac{7}{4} \times \frac{4}{4} = \frac{28}{16}$$

$$\frac{9}{16} + \frac{8}{16} + \frac{28}{16} = \frac{45}{16}$$

34. To add fractions, make sure that they have a common denominator. Since 3 is a factor of 6, 6 can be the common denominator:

$$\frac{2}{3} \times \frac{2}{2} = \frac{4}{6}$$

Now, add the numerators:

$$\frac{4}{6} + \frac{1}{6} = \frac{5}{6} \text{ of a can}$$

35. The first step here is to simplify the fraction:

$$\frac{8}{18} = \frac{4}{9}$$

Now it's clear that the fraction is a multiple of $\frac{1}{9}$, so you can easily find the decimal using a value you already know:

$$\frac{4}{9} = \frac{1}{9} \times 4 = 0.\overline{11} \times 4 = 0.\overline{44}$$

36. None of the tricks above will work for this fraction, so you need to do long division:

$$
\begin{array}{r}
0.1875 \\
16\overline{)\,3.0000} \\
-\ 1.6000 \\
\hline
1.40 \\
-\ 1.28 \\
\hline
0.120 \\
-\ 0.112 \\
\hline
0.0080 \\
-\ 0.0080 \\
\hline
0.0000
\end{array}
$$

The decimal will go in front of the answer, so now you know that $\frac{3}{16} = 0.1875$.

37. The last number in the decimal is in the hundredths place, so we can easily set up a fraction:

$$0.45 = \frac{45}{100}$$

The next step is simply to reduce the fraction down to the lowest common denominator. Here, both 45 and 100 are divisible by 5: 45 divided by 5 is 9, and 100 divided by 5 is 20. Therefore, you're left with:

$$\frac{45}{100} = \frac{9}{20}$$

38. We know that there are 5 Democrats for every 4 Republicans in the room, which means for every 9 people, 4 are Republicans:

$$5 + 4 = 9$$

Fraction of Democrats: $\frac{5}{9}$

Fraction of Republicans: $\frac{4}{9}$

If $\frac{4}{9}$ of the 90 voters are Republicans, then:

$$\frac{4}{9} \times 90 = 40 \text{ voters are Republicans}$$

39. To solve this ratio problem, we can simply multiply both sides of the ratio by the desired value to find the number of students that corresponds to having 38 teachers:

$$\frac{15 \text{ students}}{1 \text{ teacher}} \times 38 \text{ teachers} = 570$$

The school has 570 students.

40. Start by setting up the proportion:

$$\frac{120 \text{ mi}}{3 \text{ hours}} = \frac{180 \text{ mi}}{x \text{ hours}}$$

Note that it does not matter which value is placed in the numerator or denominator as long as it is the same on both sides. Now, solve for the missing quantity through cross-multiplication:

$$120 \text{ mi} \times x \text{ hr} = 3 \text{ hrs} \times 180 \text{ mi}$$

Now solve the equation:

$$x \text{ hours} = \frac{3 \text{ hrs} \times 180 \text{ mi}}{120 \text{ mi}}$$

$$x = 4.5 \text{ hrs}$$

41. Set up the equation:

$$\frac{1 \text{ acre}}{500 \text{ gal}} = \frac{x \text{ acres}}{2600 \text{ gal}}$$

Then solve for x:

$$x \text{ acres} = \frac{1 \text{ acre} \times 2600 \text{ gal}}{500 \text{ gal}}$$

$$x = \frac{26}{5} \text{ acres or } 5.2 \text{ acres}$$

42. This problem presents two equivalent ratios that can be set up in a fraction equation:

$$\frac{35}{5} = \frac{49}{x}$$

You can then cross-multiply to solve for x:

$$35x = 49 \times 5$$

$$x = 7$$

43. Set up the appropriate equation and solve; do not forget to change 15% to a decimal value:

$$whole = \frac{part}{percent} = \frac{45}{0.15} = 300$$

44. Set up the appropriate equation and solve:

$$whole = \frac{part}{percent} = \frac{15 + 30 + 20}{0.30} = 217$$

45. Set up the equation and solve:

$$percent = \frac{part}{whole} = \frac{39}{65} = 0.6 \text{ or } 60\%$$

46. You can use the information in the question to figure out what percentage of subscriptions were sold by Max and Greta:

$$percent = \frac{part}{whole} = \frac{51 + 45}{240} = \frac{96}{240} = 0.4 \text{ or } 40\%$$

However, the question asks how many subscriptions were NOT sold by Max or Greta. If Max and Greta sold a combined 40% of that month's subscriptions, then the other salespeople sold:

$$100\% - 40\% = 60\%$$

47. Set up the equation and solve; remember to convert 75% to a decimal value: $part = whole \times percent = 45 \times 0.75 = 33.75$, so Grant needs to answer at least 34 questions correctly.

48. Set up the appropriate equation and solve:

$$amount\ of\ change = original\ amount \times percent\ change$$

$$25 \times 0.4 = 10$$

If the amount of change is 10, that means the store adds a markup of $10, so the game costs:

$$\$25 + \$10 = \$35$$

49. First, calculate the amount of change:

$$75 - 40 = 35$$

Now you can set up the equation and solve. (Note that the term *markup rate* is another term for *percent change*):

$$percent\ change = \frac{amount\ of\ change}{original\ amount}$$

$$\frac{35}{40} = 0.875 = 87.5\%$$

50. You are solving for the original price, but it is going to be tricky because you do not know the amount of price change; you only know the new price. To solve, you need to create an expression for the amount of change:

If $original\ amount = x$, then $amount\ of\ change = 63 - x$. Now you can plug these values into your equation:

$$original\ amount = \frac{amount\ of\ change}{percent\ change}$$

$$x = \frac{63 - x}{0.4}$$

The last step is to solve for x:

$$0.4x = 63 - x$$

$$1.4x = 63$$

$$x = 45$$

The store paid $45 for the shoes.

51. You have been asked to find the sale price, which means you need to solve for the amount of change first:

$$amount\ of\ change = original\ amount \times percent\ change = 55 \times 0.25 = 13.75$$

Using this amount, you can find the new price. Because the item is on sale, we know that it will cost less than the original price:

$$55 - 13.75 = 41.25$$

The sale price is $41.25.

52. This problem is tricky because you need to figure out what each number in the problem stands for: 24% is obviously the percent change, but what about the measurements in feet? If you multiply these values you get the area of the garden:

$$18\ ft \times 51\ ft = 918\ ft^2$$

This 918 ft² is the amount of change—how much area the yard lost to create the garden.

Now you can set up an equation:

$$original\ amount = \frac{amount\ of\ change}{percent\ change}$$

$$\frac{918}{0.24} = 3825$$

If the original lawn was 3825 ft², and the garden is 918 ft², then the remaining area is: $3825 - 918 = 2907$. The remaining lawn covers 2907 ft².

53. These numbers are in different formats—one is a mixed fraction and the other is just a fraction. So, the first step is to convert the mixed fraction to a fraction:

$$4\frac{3}{4} = \frac{4 \times 4}{4} + \frac{3}{4} = \frac{19}{4}$$

Once the mixed number is converted, it is easier to see that $\frac{19}{4}$ is greater than $\frac{18}{4}$.

54. These numbers are already in the same format, so the decimal values just need to be compared. Remember that zeros can be added after the decimal without changing the value, so the three numbers can be rewritten as:

104.56

104.50

104.60

From this list, it is clear that 104.60 is the greatest because 0.60 is larger than 0.50 and 0.56.

55. The first step is to convert the numbers into the same format—65% is the same as $\frac{65}{100}$. Next, the fractions need to be converted to have the same denominator because it is difficult to compare fractions with different denominators. Using a factor of $\frac{5}{5}$ on the second fraction will give common denominators:

$\frac{13}{20} \times \frac{5}{5} = \frac{65}{100}$. It is now easy to see that the numbers are equivalent.

56. When multiplying exponents in which the base number is the same, simply add the powers:

$$2^4 \times 2^2 = 2^{4+2} = 2^6$$

$$2^6 = 2 \times 2 \times 2 \times 2 \times 2 \times 2 = 64$$

57. When an exponent is raised to a power, multiply the powers:

$$(3^4)^{-1} = 3^{-4}$$

When the exponent is a negative number, rewrite as the reciprocal of the positive exponent:

$$3^{-4} = \frac{1}{3^4}$$

$$\frac{1}{3^4} = \frac{1}{3 \times 3 \times 3 \times 3} = \frac{1}{81}$$

58. When the power is a fraction, rewrite as a radical:

$$\left(\frac{9}{4}\right)^{\frac{1}{2}} = \sqrt{\frac{9}{4}}$$

Next, distribute the radical to the numerator and denominator:

$$\sqrt{\frac{9}{4}} = \frac{\sqrt{9}}{\sqrt{4}} = \frac{3}{2}$$

59. Add each corresponding number:

$$\begin{bmatrix} 6+5 & 4+(-3) & (-8)+(-2) \\ (-3)+(-3) & 1+4 & 0+9 \end{bmatrix} = \begin{bmatrix} 11 & 1 & -10 \\ -6 & 5 & 9 \end{bmatrix}$$

60. Add each corresponding number to create two equations:

$$\begin{bmatrix} x+3 & 6+2 \\ 4+8 & y+(-1) \end{bmatrix} = \begin{bmatrix} 11 & 8 \\ 12 & 4 \end{bmatrix}$$

$$x + 3 = 11$$

$$y - 1 = 4$$

Now, solve each equation:

$$x = 8, y = 5$$

61. First, check to see that they can be multiplied: A has 3 columns and B has 3 rows, so they can. The resulting matrix will be 2×2. Now multiply the numbers in the first row of A by the numbers in the first column of B and add the results:

$$\begin{bmatrix} 1 & 3 & 0 \\ 6 & 2 & 4 \end{bmatrix} \times \begin{bmatrix} 5 & 3 \\ 2 & 1 \\ 4 & 7 \end{bmatrix} = \begin{bmatrix} (1 \times 5) + (3 \times 2) + (0 \times 4) & \square \\ \square & \square \end{bmatrix} = \begin{bmatrix} 11 & \square \\ \square & \square \end{bmatrix}$$

Now, multiply and add t find the 3 missing values:

$$\begin{bmatrix} 1 & 3 & 0 \\ 6 & 2 & 4 \end{bmatrix} \times \begin{bmatrix} 5 & 3 \\ 2 & 1 \\ 4 & 7 \end{bmatrix} =$$

$$\begin{bmatrix} (1 \times 5) + (3 \times 2) + (0 \times 4) & (1 \times 3) + (3 \times 1) + (0 \times 7) \\ (6 \times 5) + (2 \times 2) + (4 \times 4) & (6 \times 3) + (2 \times 1) + (4 \times 7) \end{bmatrix} = \begin{bmatrix} 11 & 6 \\ 50 & 48 \end{bmatrix}$$

62. Multiply each value inside the matrix by $6x$:

$$6x \begin{bmatrix} 2 & -3 \\ 6 & 4 \end{bmatrix} = \begin{bmatrix} 6x \times 2 & 6x \times (-3) \\ 6x \times 6 & 6x \times 4 \end{bmatrix} = \begin{bmatrix} 12x & -18x \\ 36x & 24x \end{bmatrix}$$

Chapter 4

1. Plug in each number for the correct variable and simplify:

$$2x + 6y - 3z = 2(2) + 6(4) - 3(-3) = 4 + 24 + 9 = 37$$

2. Start by grouping together like terms:

$$(5xy + 11xy) + (2yz - 5yz) + 7y$$

Now you can add together each set of like terms:

$$16xy + 7y - 3yz$$

3. Multiply the coefficients and variables together:

$$3 \times 2 = 6$$

$$y^2 \times y^4 = y^6$$

$$z \times z^5 = z^6$$

Now put all the terms back together:

$$6x^4 y^6 z^6$$

4. Multiply each term inside the parentheses by the term $2y^2$:

$$(2y^2)(y^3 + 2xy^2z + 4z) =$$

$$(2y^2 \times y^3) + (2y^2 \times 2xy^2z) + (2y^2 \times 4z) = 2y^5 + 4xy^4z + 8y^2z$$

5. Use the acronym *FOIL*—first, outer, inner, last—to multiply the terms:

---

first: $5x \times 3x = 15x^2$

outer: $5x \times 3 = 15x$

inner: $2 \times 3x = 6x$

last: $2 \times 3 = 6$

Now combine like terms:

$$15x^2 + 21x + 6$$

6. Simplify by looking at each variable and checking for those that appear in the numerator and denominator:

$$\frac{2}{8} = \frac{1}{4}$$

$$\frac{x^4}{x^2} = \frac{x^2}{1}$$

$$\frac{z}{z^2} = \frac{1}{z}$$

$$\frac{2x^4 y^3 z}{8x^2 z^2} = \frac{x^2 y^3}{4z}$$

7. First, find the highest common factor. Both terms are divisible by 9:

$\frac{27x^2}{9} = 3x^2$ and $\frac{9x}{9} = x$

Now the expression is $9(3x^2 - x)$. But wait, you're not done! Both terms can be divided by x:

$\frac{3x^2}{x} = 3x$ and $\frac{x}{x} = 1$

The final factored expression is $9x(3x-1)$.

8. Since there is no obvious factor by which you can divide terms, you should consider whether this expression fits one of the polynomial identities. This expression is a difference of squares: $a^2 - b^2$, where $a^2 = 25x^2$ and $b^2 = 16$.

Recall that $a^2 - b^2 = (a + b)(a - b)$; now solve for a and b:

$$a = \sqrt{25x^2} = 5x$$

$$b = \sqrt{16} = 4$$

$$(a + b)(a-b) = (5x + 4)(5x-4)$$

You can check your work by using the FOIL acronym to expand your answer back to the original expression:

first: $5x \times 5x = 25x^2$

outer: $5x \times -4 = -20x$

inner: $4 \times 5x = 20x$

last: $4 \times -4 = -16$

$$25x^2 - 20x + 20x - 16 = 25x^2 - 16$$

9. This is another polynomial identity, $a^2 + 2ab + b^2$. (The more you practice these problems, the faster you will recognize polynomial identities.)

$a^2 = 100x^2$, $2ab = 60x$, and $b^2 = 9$

Recall that $a^2 + 2ab + b^2 = (a + b)^2$.

Now solve for a and b:

$$a = \sqrt{100x^2} = 10x$$

$$b = \sqrt{9} = 3$$

(Double check your work by confirming that $2ab = 2 \times 10x \times 3 = 60x$)

$$(a + b)^2 = (10x + 3)^2$$

10. This equation has no parentheses, fractions, or like terms on the same side, so you can start by subtracting 12 from both sides of the equation:

$$25x + 12 = 62$$

$$(25x + 12) - 12 = 62 - 12$$

$$25x = 50$$

Now, divide by 25 to isolate the variable:

$$\frac{25x}{25} = \frac{50}{25}$$

$$x = 2$$

11. Start by distributing to get rid of the parentheses (do not forget to distribute the negative):

$$2x - 4(2x + 3) = 24$$

$$2x - 8x - 12 = 24$$

There are no fractions, so now you can join like terms:

$$2x - 8x - 12 = 24$$

$$-6x - 12 = 24$$

Now add 12 to both sides and divide by −6.

$$-6x - 12 = 24$$

$$(-6x - 12) + 12 = 24 + 12$$

$$-6x = 36$$

$$\frac{-6x}{-6} = \frac{36}{-6}$$

$$x = -6$$

12. Start by multiplying by the least common denominator to get rid of the fractions:

$$\frac{x}{3} + \frac{1}{2} = \frac{x}{6} - \frac{5}{12}$$

$$12(\frac{x}{3} + \frac{1}{2}) = 12(\frac{x}{6} - \frac{5}{12})$$

$$4x + 6 = 2x - 5$$

Now you can isolate the x:

$$(4x + 6) - 6 = (2x - 5) - 6$$

$$4x = 2x - 11$$

$$(4x) - 2x = (2x - 11) - 2x$$

$$2x = -11$$

$$x = -\frac{11}{2}$$

13. This equation looks more difficult because it has 2 variables, but you can use the same steps to solve for x. First, distribute to get rid of the parentheses and combine like terms:

$$2(x + y) - 7x = 14x + 3$$

$$2x + 2y - 7x = 14x + 3$$

$$-5x + 2y = 14x + 3$$

Now you can move the x terms to one side and everything else to the other, and then divide to isolate x:

$$-5x + 2y = 14x + 3$$

$$-19x = -2y + 3$$

$$x = \frac{2y - 3}{19}$$

14. Slope is easiest to find when the equation is in point-slope form: ($y = mx + b$). Rearrange the equation to isolate y:

$$\frac{3y}{2} + 3 = x$$

$$3y + 6 = 2x$$

$$y + 2 = \frac{2x}{3}$$

$$y = \frac{2x}{3} - 2$$

Finally, identify the term m to find the slope of the line:

$$m = \frac{2}{3}$$

15. First, rearrange the linear equation to point-slope form:

$$y = mx + b$$
$$2y - 4x = 6$$
$$y = 2x + 3$$

Next, identify the y-intercept (b) and the slope (m):

$b = 3, m = 2$

Now, plot the y-intercept $(0, b) = (0, 3)$:

Next, plug in values for x and solve for y:

$$y = 2(1) + 3 = 5 \;\rightarrow\; (1, 5)$$
$$y = 2(-1) + 3 = 1 \;\rightarrow\; (-1, 1)$$

Plot these points on the graph, and connect the points with a straight line:

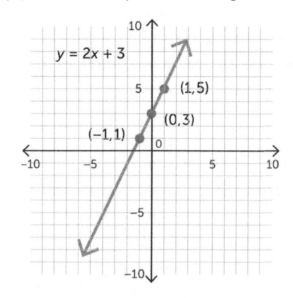

16. To solve this system using substitution, first solve one equation for a single variable:

$$3y - 4 + x = 0$$
$$3y + x = 4$$
$$x = 4 - 3y$$

Next, substitute the expression to the right of the equal sign for x in the second equation:

$$5x + 6y = 11$$
$$5(4 - 3y) + 6y = 11$$
$$20 - 15y + 6y = 11$$
$$20 - 9y = 11$$
$$-9y = -9$$
$$y = 1$$

Finally, plug the value for y back into the first equation to find the value of x:

$$3y - 4 + x = 0$$
$$3(1) - 4 + x = 0$$
$$-1 + x = 0$$
$$x = 1$$

The solution is $x = 1$ and $y = 1$, or the point (1, 1).

17. To solve this system using elimination, start by manipulating one equation so that a variable (in this case x) will cancel when the equations are added together:

$$2x + 4y = 8$$
$$-2(2x + 4y = 8)$$
$$-4x - 8y = -16$$

Now you can add the two equations together, and the x variable will drop out:

$$-4x - 8y = -16$$
$$4x + 2y = 10$$
$$-6y = -6$$
$$y = 1$$

Lastly, plug the y value into one of the equations to find the value of x:

$$2x + 4y = 8$$
$$2x + 4(1) = 8$$
$$2x + 4 = 8$$
$$2x = 4$$
$$x = 2$$

The solution is $x = 2$ and $y = 1$, or the point (2, 1).

18. Start by building an equation. David's amount will be d, Jesse's amount will be j, and Mark's amount will be m. All three must add up to $100:

$$d + j + m = 100$$

It may seem like there are three unknowns in this situation, but you can express j and m in terms of d:

Jesse gets $10 less than David, so $j = d - 10$.

Mark gets $15 less than Jesse, so $m = j - 15$.

Substitute the previous expression for j to solve for m in terms of d:

$$m = (d - 10) - 15 = d - 25$$

Now back to our original equation, substituting for j and m:

$$d + (d - 10) + (d - 25) = 100$$
$$3d - 35 = 100$$
$$3d = 135$$
$$d = 45$$

David will get $45.

19. Start by building an equation. One of the numbers in question will be x. The three numbers are consecutive, so if x is the smallest number then the other two numbers must be $(x + 1)$ and $(x + 2)$. You know that the sum of the three numbers is 54: $x + (x + 1) + (x + 2) = 54$

Now solve for the equation to find x:

$$3x + 3 = 54$$
$$3x = 51$$
$$x = 17$$

The question asks about the middle number $(x + 1)$, so the answer is 18.

Notice that you could have picked any number to be x. If you picked the middle number as x, your equation would be $(x - 1) + x + (x + 1) = 54$. Solve for x to get 18.

20. This word problem might seem complicated at first, but as long as you keep your variables straight and translate the words into mathematical operations you can easily build an equation. The quantity you want to solve is the number of girls on the swim team, so this will be x. The number of boys on the swim team will be y.

There are 6 fewer boys than girls so $y = x - 6$.

The total number of boys and girls on the swim team is $x + y$.

42 is 8 more than half this number, so $42 = 8 + (x + y) \div 2$

Now substitute for y to solve for x:

$$42 = 8 + (x + x - 6) \div 2$$
$$34 = (2x - 6) \div 2$$
$$68 = 2x - 6$$
$$74 = 2x$$
$$x = 37$$

There are 37 girls on the swim team.

21. Collect like terms on each side as you would for a regular equation:

$$-7x + 2 < 6 - 5x$$

$$-2x < 4$$

When you divide by a negative number, the direction of the sign switches: $-2x < 4 = x > -2$

22. To rearrange the inequality into $y = mx + b$ form, first subtract 4 from both sides:

$$-3x - 4 \geq -y$$

Next divide both sides by –1 to get positive y; remember to switch the direction of the inequality symbol:

$$3x + 4 \leq y$$

Now plot the line $y = 3x + 4$, making a solid line, and then shade the side above the line:

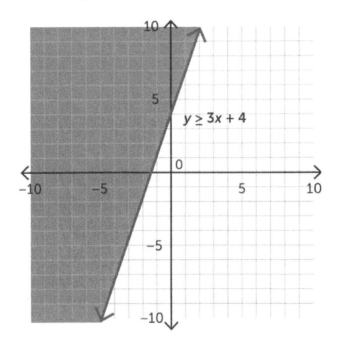

23. Not every quadratic equation you see will be presented in the standard form. Rearrange terms to set one side equal to 0: $2x2 + 14x = 0$.

Note that $a = 2$, $b = 14$, and $c = 0$ because there is no third term. Now divide the expression on the left by the common factor: $(2x)(x + 7) = 0$.

To find the roots, set each of the factors equal to 0:

$$2x = 0 \rightarrow x = 0$$

$$x + 7 = 0 \rightarrow x = -7$$

24. First rearrange the equation to set one side equal to 0:

$$3x^2 - 7x + 2 = 0$$

Next identify the terms a, b, and c:

$$a = 3$$

$$b = -7$$

$$c = 2$$

$$x = \frac{-b \pm \sqrt{b^2 - 4ac}}{2a}$$

$$x = \frac{7 \pm \sqrt{b^2 - 4ac}}{2(3)}$$

$$x = \frac{7 \pm \sqrt{25}}{6}$$

$$x = \frac{7 \pm 5}{6}$$

Since the determinant is positive, you can expect two real numbers for x. Solve for the two possible answers:

$$x = \frac{7 + 5}{6} \rightarrow x = 2$$

$$x = \frac{7 - 5}{6} \rightarrow x = -\frac{1}{3}$$

25. First, find the axis of symmetry. The equation for the line of symmetry is $x = \frac{-b}{2a}$.

$$x = \frac{-4}{2(1)} = -2$$

Next, plug in −2 for x to find the y coordinate of the vertex:

$$y = (-2)2 + 4(-2) + 1 = -3$$

The vertex is $(-2, -3)$.

Now, make a table of points on either side of the vertex by plugging in numbers for x and solving for y: x:

x	$y = x^2 + 4x + 1$	(x, y)
−3	$y = (-3)^2 + 4(-3) + 1 = -2$	$(-3, -2)$
−1	$y = (-1)^2 + 4(-1) + 1 = -2$	$(-1, -2)$
−4	$y = (-4)^2 + 4(-4) + 1 = 1$	$(-4, 1)$
0	$y = 0^2 + 4(0) + 1 = 1$	$(0, 1)$

Finally, draw the axis of symmetry, plot the vertex and your table of points, and trace the parabola:

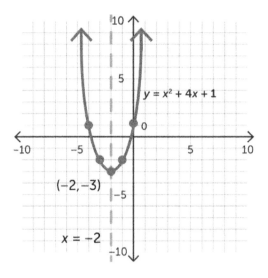

26. Plug in 9 for x:

$$f(9) = 2(9) - 10$$

$$f(9) = 8$$

27. The function $f(x)$ has a range of only positive numbers, since x cannot be negative. The function $g(x)$ has a range of positive and negative numbers, since x can be either positive or negative. The number –2, therefore, must be in the range for $g(x)$ but not for $f(x)$.

28. First, estimate the shape and direction of the graph based on the value of a. Since $a > 1$, you know that $f(x)$ will approach infinity as x increases and there will be a horizontal asymptote along the negative x-axis. Next, plot the points $(0, 1)$ and $(1, a)$. Finally, plug in one or two more values for x, plot those points and trace the graph:

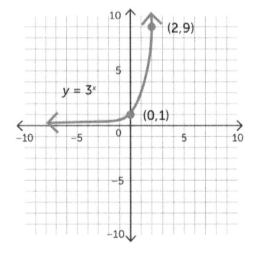

$$f(2) = 3^2 = 9 \rightarrow (2, 9)$$

29. $64 = 2^x$

The inverse of an exponent is a log. Take the log of both sides to solve for x:

$$\log_2 64 = x$$

$$x = 6$$

30. First, estimate the shape and direction of the graph based on the value of a. Since $a > 1$, you know that $f(x)$ will approach infinity as x increases and there will be a vertical asymptote along the negative y-axis.

Next, plot the points $(1, 0)$ and $(a, 1)$.

Finally, it is easier to plug in a value for $f(x)$ and solve for x rather than attempting to solve for $f(x)$. Plug in one or two values for $f(x)$, plot those points and trace the graph:

$$2 = \log_4 x$$

$$4^2 = x$$

$$16 = x \rightarrow (16, 2)$$

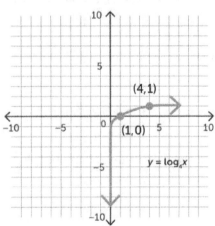

31. Rewrite the function in exponent form

$$x = \frac{1}{3}^{f(x)}$$

$$81 = \frac{1}{3}^{f(x)}$$

The question is asking: to what power must you raise $\frac{1}{3}$ to get 81?

Recognize that $3^4 = 81$, so $\frac{1^4}{3} = \frac{1}{81}$

Switch the sign of the exponent to flip the numerator and denominator:

$$\frac{1^{-4}}{3} = \frac{81}{1}$$

$$f(81) = -4$$

32. Find the difference between two terms that are next to each other: $5 - (-1) = -6$. The common difference is −6. (It must be negative to show the difference is subtracted, not added.)

Now subtract 6 from the last term to find the next term: $-13 - 6 = -19$ The next term is −19.

33. First, decide whether this is an arithmetic or geometric sequence. Since the numbers are getting farther and farther apart, you know this must be a geometric sequence. Divide one term by the term before it to find the common ratio: $18 \div 6 = 3$.

Next, plug in the common ratio and the first term to the equation $a_n = a_1(r^n)$: $a_{12} = 2(3^{12})$

$$a_{12} = 1{,}062{,}882$$

Notice that it would have taken a very long time to multiply each term by 3 until you got the twelfth term—this is where that equation comes in handy!

34. To answer this question, you can simply add $9 + 11 = 20$ to get the fifth term, $20 + 11 = 31$ to get the 6th term, and so on until you get the tenth term. Or, you can plug the information you know into your equation $a_n = a_1 + (n - 1)d$. In this case, you do not know the first term. If you use the fourth term instead, you must replace $(n - 1)$ with $(n - 4)$: $a_{10} = 9 + (10 - 4)11$

$$a_{10} = 75$$

35. Set up the first equation by removing the absolute value symbol then solve for x:

$$|2x - 3| = x + 1$$
$$2x - 3 = x + 1$$
$$x = 4$$

For the second equation, remove the absolute value and multiply by −1:

$$|2x - 3| = x + 1$$
$$2x - 3 = -(x + 1)$$
$$2x - 3 = -x - 1$$
$$3x = 2$$
$$x = \frac{2}{3}$$

Both answers are correct, so the complete answer is $x = 4$ or $\frac{2}{3}$.

36. Set up the first equation:

$$2(y + 4) = 10$$
$$y + 4 = 5$$
$$y = 1$$

Set up the second equation. Remember to isolate the absolute value before multiplying by −1:

$$2|y + 4| = 10$$
$$|y + 4| = 5$$
$$y + 4 = -5$$
$$y = -9$$
$$y = 1 \text{ or } -9$$

37. Start by listing all of the data and defining the variable:

- total number of backpacks = 48
- cost of backpacks = $476.00
- backpacks sold in store at price of $18 = 17
- backpacks sold to school at a price of $15 = 48 − 17 = 31
- total profit = x

Now set up an equation:

$$income - cost = total\ profit$$
$$(306 + 465) - 476 = 295$$

The store owner made a profit of $295.

38. Start by listing all the data and defining your variables. Note that the number of students, while given in the problem, is not needed to find the answer:

$$time\ on\ 1st\ day = \frac{3}{5}\ of\ an\ hour = 36\ min.$$

$$time\ on\ 2nd\ day = \frac{1}{2}(36) = 18\ min.$$

$$total\ time = x$$

Now set up the equation and solve:

$$total\ time = time\ on\ 1st\ day + time\ on\ 2nd\ day$$
$$x = 36 + 18 = 54$$

The students had 54 minutes to work on the projects.

39. The first step is to set up a table and fill in a value for each variable:

	d	r	t
driving	d	30	t
flying	$150 - d$	60	$3 - t$

You can now set up equations for driving and flying. The first row gives the equation $d = 30t$ and the second row gives the equation $150 - d = 60(3 - t)$.

Next, solve this system of equations. Start by substituting for d in the second equation:

$$d = 30t$$

$$150 - d = 60(3 - t)$$

$$150 - 30t = 60(3 - t)$$

Now solve for t:

$$150 - 30t = 180 - 60t - 30 = -30t$$

$$1 = t$$

Although you have solved for t, you are not done yet. Notice that the problem asks for distance. So, you need to solve for d: what the problem asked for. It does not ask for time, but you need to calculate time in order to solve the problem:

driving: $30t = 30$ miles

flying: $150 - d = 120$ miles

The distance from the airport to the hospital is 120 miles.

40. First, set up the table. The variable for time will be the same for each, because they will have been on the field for the same amount of time when they meet:

	d	r	t
horse #1	d	14	t
horse #2	$45 - d$	16	t

Next, set up two equations:

Horse #1: $d = 14t$

Horse #2: $45 - d = 16t$

Now substitute and solve:

$$d = 14t$$

$$45 - d = 16t$$

$$45 - 14t = 16t$$

$$45 = 30t$$

$$t = 1.5$$

The horses will meet 1.5 hr. after they begin.

41. Start by figuring out how much of a house the siblings can each clean on their own.

Bridget can clean the house in 12 hours, so she can clean $\frac{1}{12}$ of the house in an hour. Using the same logic, Tom can clean $\frac{1}{8}$ of a house in an hour. By adding these values together, you get the fraction of the house they can clean together in an hour:

$$\frac{1}{12} + \frac{1}{8} = \frac{5}{24}$$

They can do $\frac{5}{24}$ of the job per hour.

Now set up variables and an equation to solve:

$$t = \text{time spent cleaning (in hours)}$$

$$h = \text{number of houses cleaned} = 2$$

$$work = rate \times time$$

$$h = \frac{5}{24}t$$

$$2 = \frac{5}{24}t$$

$$t = \frac{48}{5} = 9\frac{3}{5} \text{ hr}$$

42. In this problem you do not know the exact time, but you can still find the hourly rate as a variable:

The first hose completes the job in f hours, so it waters $\frac{1}{f}$ fields per hour. The slow hose waters the field in $1.25f$, so it waters the field in $\frac{1}{1.25f}$ hours. Together, they take 5 hours to water the field, so they water $\frac{1}{5}$ of the field per hour. Now you can set up the equations and solve:

$$\frac{1}{f} + \frac{1}{1.25f} = \frac{1}{5}$$

$$1.25f\left(\frac{1}{f} + \frac{1}{1.25f}\right) = 1.25f\left(\frac{1}{5}\right)$$

$$1.25 + 1 = 0.25f$$

$$f = 9$$

The fast hose takes 9 hours to water the field. The slow hose takes $1.25(9) = 11.25$ hours.

43. Calculate how many apples each person can pick per hour:

Ben: $\dfrac{500\ apples}{2\ hr.} = \dfrac{250\ apples}{hr.}$

Frank: $\dfrac{450\ apples}{3\ hr.} = \dfrac{150\ apples}{hr.}$

Together: $\dfrac{250+150\ apples}{hr.} = \dfrac{400\ apples}{hr.}$

Now, set up an equation to find the time it takes to pick 1,000 apples:

$$Total\ time = \frac{1\ hr.}{400\ apples} \times 1,000$$

$$apples = \frac{1,000}{400\ hr.} = 2.5\ hours$$

Chapter 5

1. The perimeter of a rectangle is equal to twice its length plus twice its width:

$$P = 2(20) + 2(28) = 96\ m$$

The farmer has 100 meters of fencing, so he'll have

$100 - 96 = 4$ meters left.

2. Each side of the square wall is 3.5 meters:

$$A = 3.5^2 = 12.25m^2$$

Approximately 16.8 cubic centimeters of water spilled out of the fishbowl.

3. This question is asking about the volume of Charlotte's pool. The circular pool is actually a cylinder, so use the formula for a cylinder:

$$V = \pi r\ 2h.$$

The diameter is 6 meters. The radius is half the diameter so r = 6 ÷ 2 = 3 meters.

Now solve for the volume:

$$V = \pi r 2h$$

$$V = \pi (3\ m)2(1\ m)$$

$$V = 28.3\ m3$$

Charlotte will need approximately 28�3 cubic meters of water to fill her pool.

4. Since the fishbowl was filled to the brim, the volume of the water that spilled out of it is equal to the volume of the marbles that Danny dropped into it. First, find the volume of one marble using the equation for a sphere:

$$V = 4\pi r^3$$

$$V = 4\pi (1\ cm)^3$$

$$V = 4.2\ cm^3$$

Since Danny dropped in 4 marbles, multiply this volume by 4 to find the total volume:

$$4.2\ cm^3 \times 4 = 16.8\ cm\text{^}3$$

5. First divide the diameter by two to find the radius:

$$r = 10\ cm \div 2 = 5\ cm$$

Now use the formula for intercepted arc length:

$$l = 2\pi r\ \theta$$

$$l = 2\pi(5\ cm)\ 46°$$

$$l = 4.0\ cm$$

6. Use the formula for chord length: chord length $= 2\sqrt{r^2 - d^2}$

In this example, we are told the chord length and the radius, and we need to solve for d:

$$6\ cm = 2\sqrt{(5\ cm)^2 - d^2}$$

$$3\ cm = \sqrt{(5\ cm)^2 - d^2}$$

$$9\ cm^2 = 25\ cm^2 - d^2$$

$$d^2 = 16\ cm^2$$

$$d = 4\ cm$$

7. Draw out Kate's and Emily's trips to see that their routes form two triangles. The triangles have

corresponding sides with lengths of 6 miles and 8 miles, and a corresponding angle in between of 150°. This fits the "SAS" rule so the triangles must be congruent. The length Kate has to ride home corresponds to the length Emily has to ride home, so Emily must ride 12 miles.

8. For parallel lines cut by a transversal, look for vertical and corresponding angles.

Angles A and D are vertical angles, so angle D must be congruent to angle A. Angle $D = 53°$.

Angles D and H are corresponding angles, so angle H must be congruent to angle D. Angle $H = 53°$.

9. Start by drawing a picture of Erica's route. You'll see it forms a triangle:

4 miles

One leg of the triangle is missing, but you can find its length using the Pythagorean Theorem:

$$a2 + b2 = c2$$

$$32 + 42 = c2$$

$$25 = c2$$

$$c = 5$$

Adding all 3 sides gives the length of the whole race:

$$3 + 4 + 5 = 12\ miles$$

10. Draw a triangle with the known length and angle labeled.

The known side (the length of the ladder) is the hypotenuse of the triangle, and the unknown distance is the side opposite the angle. Therefore, you can use sine:

$$\sin\theta = \frac{opposite}{hypotenuse}$$

$$sin15°(20\ feet)$$

Now solve for the opposite side:

$$opposite = sin15°(20\ feet)$$

$$opposite = 5.2\ feet$$

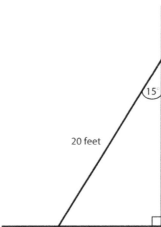

11. Draw a diagram and notice that the line from Grace's eyes to the hoop of the basket forms the hypotenuse of a right triangle. The side adjacent to the angle of her eyes is the distance from the basket: 8 feet. The side opposite to Grace's eyes is the difference between the height of her eyes and the height of the basket: 10 feet – 5 feet = 5 feet.

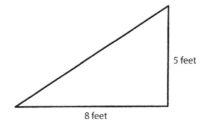

Next, use the formula for tangent to solve for the angle:

opposite

adjacent

$$tan\theta = \frac{opposite}{adjacent}$$

$$tan\theta = \frac{5ft}{8ft}$$

Now take the inverse tangent of both sides to solve for the angle:

$$\theta = tan^{-1}\frac{5}{8}$$

$$\theta = 32°$$

12. To find the coordinates, you must find Matt's displacement along the x- and y-axes. Matt hiked 1 mile north and zero miles south, so his displacement along the

y-axis is +1 mile. Matt hiked 2 miles east and 3 miles west, so his displacement along the x-axis is + 2 miles – 3 miles = –1 mile.

Matt's coordinates are (−1,1).

13. Draw the coordinate plane and plot the given points. If you connect these points you will see that the bottom side is 6 units long. Since it is a square, all sides must be 6 units long. Count 6 units up from the point (4,3) to find the top right corner.

The coordinates for the top right corner are (4,9).

14. Plug the values for x 1,x 2,y 1,and y2 into the distance formula and simplify:

$$d = \sqrt{(-5-3)^2 + \left(2-(-6)\right)^2} =$$

$$\sqrt{64+64} = \sqrt{64 \times 2} = 8\sqrt{2}$$

15. Plug the values for x 1, x 2, y 1, and y2 into the midpoint formula and simplify:

$$midpoint = \left(\frac{3+(-5)}{2}, \frac{(-6)+2}{2}\right)$$

$$= (\frac{-2}{2}, \frac{-4}{2}) = (-1,-2)$$

Chapter 6

1. Add the terms, then divide by the number of terms:

$$mean = \frac{24+27+18}{3} = 23$$

2. Set up the equation for mean with x representing the third number, then solve:

$$mean = \frac{38+43+x}{3} = 45$$

$$\frac{38+43+x}{3} = 45$$

$$38+43+x = 135$$

$$x = 54$$

3. Place the terms in order, then pick the middle term:

18, 24, 27

The median is 24.

4. Place the terms in order. Because there is an even number of terms, the median will be the average of the middle 2 terms:

18, 19, 24, 27

$$median = \frac{19+24}{2} = 21.5$$

5. The mode is 2 because it appears the most within the set.

6. To find the standard deviation, first find the mean:

$$mean = 62 + 63 + 61 + 66 = 63$$

Next, find the difference between each term and the mean, and square that number:

$$63 - 62 = 1 \rightarrow 12 = 1$$
$$63 - 63 = 0 \rightarrow 02 = 0$$
$$63 - 61 = 2 \rightarrow 22 - 4$$
$$63 - 66 = -3 \rightarrow (-3)2 = 9$$

Now, find the mean of the squares:

$$mean = \frac{1 + 0 + 4 + 9}{4} = 3.5$$

Finally, find the square root of the mean:

$$\sqrt{3.5} = 1.87$$

The standard deviation is 1.87.

7. The shortest bar will be the month that had the least rain, and the longest bar will correspond to the month with the greatest amount: July 2003 had the least, and June 2002 had the most.

8. Tracing from the top of each bar to the scale on the left shows that sales in July were 20 and September sales were 15. So, 5 more cones were sold in July.

9. 15 students have birthdays in the spring and 12 in winter, so there are 27 students with birthdays in spring or summer.

10. Use the equation for percent:

$$percent = \frac{prat}{whole} = \frac{winter\ birthdays}{total\ birthdays}$$

$$\frac{20}{20 + 15 + 23 + 12} = \frac{20}{70} = \frac{2}{7} = .286$$

Or 28.6%.

11. At 4:00 p.m., approximately 12 sodas and 5 coffees were sold, so more soda was sold.

12. This question is asking for the time of day with the most sales of coffee and soda combined. It is not necessary to add up sales at each time of day to find the answer. Just from looking at the graph, you can see that sales for both beverages were highest at noon, so the answer must be 12:00 p.m.

13. To find the total number, we need to add the number of cars for each relevant time period (note that all number are approximations):

8:00 a.m. – 11:00 a.m.: 50 cars

11:00 a.m. – 2:00 p.m.: 30 cars

2:00 p.m. – 5:00 p.m.: 35 cars

$$50 + 30 + 35 = 115\ cars$$

14. Because there are 15 marbles in the bag ($3 + 5 + 7$), the total number of possible outcomes is 15. Of those outcomes, 3 would be blue marbles, which is the desired outcome. Using that information, you can set up an equation:

$$probability = \frac{desired\ outcomes}{total\ possible\ outcomes}$$

$$= \frac{3}{15} = \frac{1}{5}$$

15. Because you're solving for desired outcomes (the number of red balls), first you need to rearrange the equation:

$$probability = \frac{desired\ outcomes}{total\ possible\ outcomes}$$

$$desired\ outcomes = probablity \times total\ possible\ outcomes$$

Here, choosing a red ball is the desired outcome. The total possible outcomes are represented by the 75 total balls. There are 45 red balls in the bag.

16. In this problem, the desired outcome is a seat in either the mezzanine or balcony area, and the total possible outcomes are represented by the 230 total seats. So, you can write this equation:

$$probability = \frac{desired\ outcomes}{total\ possible\ outcomes}$$

$$= \frac{100 + 55}{230} = 0.67$$

17. Because you're solving for total possible outcomes (total number of students), first you need to rearrange the equation:

$$probability = \frac{desired\ outcomes}{total\ possible\ outcomes}$$

In this problem, you are given a probability (7% or 0.07) and the number of desired outcomes

(42). Plug these numbers into the equation to solve:

$$total\ possible\ outcomes = \frac{42}{0.07} = 600\ students$$

18. This question is asking about an intersection of events. The equation for an intersection of $P(A \cap B) = P(A) \times P(B|)$.

The first event, event A, is picking out a blue marble. Fin $P(A)$:

$$P(A) = \frac{11\ blue\ marbles}{16\ total\ marbles} = \frac{11}{16}$$

The second event, event B, is picking out a red marble, now that there are 15 marbles left. Find

$$P(B|A) = \frac{5\ red\ marbles}{15\ total\ marbles} = \frac{5}{15} = \frac{1}{3}$$

$$P(A \cap B) = P(A) \times P(B|A)$$

$$= \frac{11}{16} \times \frac{1}{3} = \frac{11}{48}$$

19. This question is asking about a union of events. The equation for a union of events is:

$$P(A \cup B) = P(A) + P(B) - P(A \cap B)$$

The first event, event A, is selecting a queen. Find P(A):

$$P(A) = \frac{4 \; queens}{52 \; total \; cards} = \frac{4}{52}$$

The second event, event B, is selecting a diamond. Find P(B):

$$P(B) = \frac{13 \; diamonds}{52 \; total \; cards} = 13$$

Now, find the probability of selecting a queen that is also a diamond:

$$P(A \cap B) = \frac{1 \; diamond \; queen}{52 \; total \; cards} = \frac{1}{52}$$

$$P(A \cup B) = P(A) + P(B) - P(A \cap B)$$

$$= \frac{4}{52} + \frac{13}{52} - \frac{1}{52} = \frac{16}{52} = \frac{4}{13}$$

Practice Test #1
Reading and Writing

For each question, choose the option that BEST answers the question related to the passage and/or graphic.

Module I

1. *Demetrius used to say that there was no difference between the words and the voice of the _____ ignorant and the sounds and noises of a stomach full of superfluous wind. And it was not without reason that he said this, for he considered it to be indifferent whence the utterance of such men proceeded, whether from their mouth or their body; both being of the same substance and value.*

Which word or phrase is the MOST logical and precise option to complete the blank in the passage?
- A) bilious
- B) resentful
- C) unskilled
- D) sickly

2. *An Imperial policy must, of course, be carried out with reasonable prudence, and the principles of government which guide our relations with whatsoever races are brought under our control must be politically and economically sound and morally defensible. This is, in fact, the keystone of the Imperial arch.*

As used in the text, what does the word prudence MOST nearly mean?
- A) caution
- B) boldness
- C) cleverness
- D) ingenuity

3. *My mistress' eyes are nothing like the sun;*

Coral is far more red, than her lips red:

If snow be white, why then her breasts are dun;

If hairs be wires, black wires grow on her head.

I have seen roses damask'd, red and white,

But no such roses see I in her cheeks;

And in some perfumes is there more delight

Than in the breath that from my mistress reeks.

I love to hear her speak, yet well I know

That music hath a far more pleasing sound:

I grant I never saw a goddess go;

My mistress, when she walks, treads on the ground:

And yet by heaven, I think my love as rare,

As any she belied with false compare.

Which answer option BEST describes the overall structure of the text?
A) It begins with flattery and moves toward realism.
B) It presents alternating descriptions of a woman's features and those of an ideal woman.
C) It sketches an unflattering portrait of a mistress who has fallen out of favor with the poet.
D) It makes a series of comparisons between the features of a woman and those of a fanciful ideal.

4. *When I had run a long way, I went into a yard, but the people there didn't like cats; a boy was sent to chase me through the gate, and I continued my wearisome journey. <u>How I did wish that somebody would take me up or show me the way home; but nobody seemed to care what became of me</u>. Finally, being so very tired, I crawled in under a fence, and seeing no one around, I lay down in the corner and went to sleep.*

Which option BEST states the function of the underlined sentence in the text as a whole?
A) It provides the reasoning for a decision made in the following sentence.
B) It elaborates on the wearisome journey noted in the previous sentence.
C) It gives insight into the mind of the protagonist in a way the rest of the passage does not.
D) It provides a counterpoint to the previous statement.

5. Text 1

When the ideal of Society is material gain or possession, as it is largely today, the object of its special condemnation is the thief—not the rich thief, for he is already in possession and therefore respectable, but the poor thief. There is nothing to show that the poor thief is really more immoral or unsocial than the respectable money-grubber; but it is very clear that the money-grubber has been floating with the great current of Society, while the poor man has been swimming against it, and so has been worsted. Or when, as today, Society rests on private property in land, its counter-ideal is the poacher.

Text 2

Leo Tolstoy greatly admired and was heavily influenced by Proudhon, considering his "property is theft" as "an absolute truth" that would "survive as long as humanity."

Based on the texts, how would Leo Tolstoy (Text 2) MOST likely view the statement that is being conveyed in the second sentence in Text 1?
- A) as oversimplifying the idea of property ownership to make it seem like an immoral act
- B) as showing a clear understanding of how society has arbitrarily decided that landowners are upstanding citizens despite their property ownership denying resources to others
- C) as disingenuously claiming that property ownership is a kind of thievery that society currently tolerates rather than a legitimate enterprise
- D) as equating the idea of property ownership with that of thievery in an inflammatory way that will not stand the test of time

6. *A food substance necessary to plant life and growth is nitrogen. Since a vast store of nitrogen exists in the air, it would seem that plants should never lack for this food, but most plants are unable to make use of the boundless store of atmospheric nitrogen because they do not possess the power of extracting nitrogen from the air. For this reason, they depend solely upon nitrogenous compounds that are present in the soil and soluble in water. The soluble nitrogenous soil compounds are absorbed by roots and are utilized by plants for food.*

Which of these actions does the text suggest would result in the healthiest plants?
- A) pumping extra nitrogen into the air
- B) supplementing nitrogenous compounds in the soil
- C) genetically engineering plants to better extract nitrogen from the air
- D) injecting nitrogen directly into the plants

7. *It was precisely in this year when men's minds were excited over the wonderful powers of the galvanic current, and a wide prospect was opened of its future advantage to men, when, indeed, the general public understood very little about the principle and were in a condition of mind to accept almost any scientific marvel, that there appeared in Paris an adventurer, who undertook to open communications between all parts of the world without the expense and difficulty of laying cables of communication. The line laid across the channel in 1850 was not very successful; it broke several times, and had to be taken up again, and re-laid in 1851.*

Which answer option BEST states the main purpose of the text?
- A) It points out how the ignorant public are too quick to assume that some novel invention will work.
- B) It explains the ways in which experiments with galvanic current fail.
- C) It presents an example of an invention that failed to live up to the promise of its public appeal.
- D) It argues that the public should not be involved in deciding which experiments to support.

8. *We quite agree that poetry is not a formula. But what does Mr. Gosse propose to do about it? If Mr. Gosse had found himself in the flood of poetastry in the reign of Elizabeth, what would he have done about it? Would he have stemmed it? What exactly is this abyss? And if something "has gone amiss with our standards," is it wholly the fault of the younger generation that it is aware of no authority that it must respect? It is part of the business of the critic to preserve tradition—_____.*

Which option MOST logically completes the text?
- A) without making statements about what about that tradition needs changing
- B) while taking care not to ruffle any feathers
- C) not to criticize as such
- D) where a good tradition exists

9. *Pride and Prejudice* is an 1813 novel by Jane Austen. In the novel, Austen portrays Mrs. Bennet's primary interest as securing satisfactory marriages for her daughters, as is evident from her response to being informed that her eldest, Jane, has caught cold while visiting Mr. Bingley at Netherfield.

Which quotation from *Pride and Prejudice* MOST effectively illustrates the above claim?
- A) *"This was a lucky idea of mine, indeed!" said Mrs. Bennet, more than once, as if the credit of making it rain were all her own. Till the next morning, however, she was not aware of all the felicity of her contrivance.*
- B) *In spite of this amendment, however, she requested to have a note sent to Longbourn, desiring her mother to visit Jane, and form her own judgment of her situation. The note was immediately dispatched, and its contents as quickly complied with. Mrs. Bennet, accompanied by her two youngest girls, reached Netherfield soon after the family breakfast.*
- C) *Had she found Jane in any apparent danger, Mrs. Bennet would have been very miserable; but being satisfied on seeing her that her illness was not alarming, she had no wish of her recovering immediately, as her restoration to health would probably remove her from Netherfield.*
- D) *"Oh dear, yes; but you must own she is very plain. Lady Lucas herself has often said so, and envied me Jane's beauty. I do not like to boast of my own child; but to be sure, Jane—one does not often see anybody better looking. It is what everybody says. I do not trust my own partiality. When she was only fifteen there was a gentleman at my brother Gardiner's in town so much in love with her, that my sister-in-law was sure he would make her an offer before we came away. But, however, he did not. Perhaps he thought her too young. However, he wrote some verses on her, and very pretty they were."*

Module I

10. Use the information below to answer the question which follows.

Participant Ratings of Level-Two Mattress Comfort		
Participant	**Comfort Rating**	**Preferred Firmness Adjustment**
18	2	firmer
3	1	firmer
7	4	firmer

Jackson conducted multiple surveys to determine participants' comfort level when sleeping on mattresses of the brand's second-lowest firmness level. Participants filled out surveys upon waking and reported their levels of comfort on a scale from 1 (very uncomfortable) to 5 (very comfortable), with 3 indicating neutral (neither uncomfortable nor comfortable), and to indicate whether they would prefer a firmer or a softer mattress. The table shows how three participants responded in their morning surveys. According to the table, all three would have preferred a firmer mattress, _____.

Which option MOST effectively uses data from the table to complete the statement?
   A)   with participant 7 expressing the least discomfort throughout the night
   B)   though seven participants expressed a high comfort level throughout the night
   C)   with twenty-one participants expressing severe discomfort
   D)   and participant 18 expressed the most discomfort throughout the night

11. *I was telling you that as I lay a-dying, I found myself endeavoring to find fitting words to describe my sensations. At this point, however, the train of my thoughts was disturbed—and I recollect a slight reawakening of my old characteristic irritability at the interruption—by the entrance of a sister who had come from a distance to see me. I remember slightly lifting my head to speak to her, and then glancing round the room to see if all were present.*

According to the text, why is the narrator irritated by the entrance of his sister?
   A)   He tends to be annoyed by interruptions to his train of thought.
   B)   He is doing something important and does not want to speak with her.
   C)   He had hoped somebody else had come to speak with him.
   D)   He was hoping not to have to deal with his sister that day.

12. *A researcher conducted an experiment to determine the most common psychological reason that Halloween haunt performers are drawn to the job, hypothesizing that these performers are mainly using these haunts as a healthy way to enjoy causing others distress. The researcher recruited several participants who had worked in multiple haunt attractions, defined as attractions in which performers are encouraged to scare visitors who are walking through, and asked them for statements about what they most enjoy about the job.*

Which quotation from a participant would MOST strongly disprove the researcher's hypothesis?
- A) "It is amazing to see people react so strongly to an aspect of your performance that they almost run out of the building."
- B) "My favorite part is seeing groups of friends laughing at each other as they run screaming from one station to the next."
- C) "Knowing that I have gotten to provide so many people with that burst of adrenaline they were craving makes me feel really happy."
- D) "I would never have gotten to use all of my character voices if I hadn't started doing haunts."

13. *Luggage is not usually carried in hermetically sealed sedan chairs, but Saint-Mars has explained why, by surplus of precaution, he did not use a litter. The litter might break down and Dauger might be seen. A new prison was built specially, at the cost of 5,000 livres, for Dauger at Sainte-Marguerite, with large sunny rooms. On May 3, 1687, Saint-Mars had entered on his island realm, Dauger being nearly killed by twelve days' journey in a closed chair.*

According to the text, what was the purpose of the closed chair in which Dauger rode to the prison?
- A) to bring the prisoner in quickly without interference from the public
- B) to prevent the prisoner from causing a stir when people saw him being transported
- C) to ensure Dauger would not be seen by the prisoner
- D) to keep Dauger from seeing the prisoner

14. *A sound of wild mirth, of snatches of song, of wrangling and shouting came to him from the pickers' quarters. He dreaded returning to ___ midst and wished that he could sleep in the little white bed at Mr. Welch's or in his own tiny room at home, instead of in one of those queer-looking bunks roughly made of boards and built along the sides of the room.*

Which option completes the text so that it conforms to the conventions of Standard English?
- A) there
- B) their
- C) they're
- D) the

15. *His shyness wore off by degrees, and he talked constantly, not of his family life, but ___ his beloved Eton, from which he appeared to have been ruthlessly torn, and of his feats at cricket. He was a champion "dry bob," he assured her proudly.*

Which option completes the text so that it conforms to the conventions of Standard English?
- A) of
- B) about
- C) for
- D) to

16. *The picturesque village of Rudge-in-the-Vale dozed in the summer sunshine. Along its narrow _____ of life visible were a cat stropping its backbone against the Jubilee Watering Trough, some flies doing deep-breathing exercises on the hot windowsills, and a little group of serious thinkers who, propped up against the wall of the Carmody Arms, were waiting for that establishment to open.*

Which option completes the text so that it conforms to the conventions of Standard English?
- A) High Street the only signs
- B) High Street: the only signs
- C) High Street, the only signs
- D) High Street; the only signs

17. *For this magnificent work, the highest credit is due to the United States chief sanitary officer, Colonel Gorgas. It is well known how the American Medical Commission in Cuba proved six years ago that yellow fever is conveyed from man to man solely and entirely by a gnat common in Central America, known as Stegomyia, and further, how by carrying out measures for preventing the entrance of these gnats into dwelling-houses, and especially _____ so that they fail to obtain and carry the yellow fever germ, even if they do bite healthy men, Colonel Gorgas and his associates practically eradicated yellow fever in Cuba.*

Which option completes the text so that it conforms to the conventions of Standard English?
- A) by keeping them away, from yellow fever patients,
- B) by keeping them away (from yellow fever patients)
- C) by keeping them away—from yellow fever patients—
- D) by keeping them away from yellow fever patients

18. *A grander and severer aspect characterizes the plains of the interior of Africa. Like the wide expanse of the Pacific Ocean, ___ only in recent times that attempts have been made to explore them thoroughly.*

Which option completes the text so that it conforms to the conventions of Standard English?
- A) it was
- B) it is
- C) it had been
- D) it will be

19. *This conquest of Gaul, during which he drove the Germans back to their forests, and inaugurated a policy of conciliation and moderation which made the Gauls the faithful allies of Rome, and ___ country its most fertile and important province, furnishing able men both for the Senate and the Army, was not only a great feat of genius, but a great service—a transcendent service—to the State, which entitled Caesar to a magnificent reward. Had it been cordially rendered to him, he might have been contented with a sort of perpetual consulship, and with the éclat of being the foremost man of the Empire.*

Which option completes the text so that it conforms to the conventions of Standard English?
- A) her
- B) his
- C) their
- D) its

20. *Under these circumstances, the English Government concluded that it was impossible that England alone, overburdened as she was by taxation, could undertake the military defense of her greatly extended Empire. Their object, _____, was to create subsidiary armies for its defense.*

Which option completes the text with the MOST logical transition?
- A) moreover
- B) however
- C) therefore
- D) in spite of this

21. *Instead of such a mass of dead protein, _____, take a particle of living protein—one of those minute microscopic living things which throng our pools, and are known as Infusoria—such a creature, for instance, as an Euglena, and place it in our vessel of water. It is a round mass provided with a long filament, and except in this peculiarity of shape, presents no appreciable physical or chemical difference whereby it might be distinguished from the particle of dead protein.*

Which option completes the text with the MOST logical transition?
- A) in fact
- B) therefore
- C) moreover
- D) however

22. While researching a topic, a student has taken the following notes:
- An investigation will usually follow a diving accident that was either fatal or could potentially result in litigation.

- The United States Coast Guard will often investigate a death involving diving from a vessel in coastal waters.

- Accidents involving specialized equipment can require greater expertise to handle properly.

- Rebreather equipment can prove especially problematic for cases run by investigators who are not diving experts.

- There is encouragement within the diving community to report "near misses" as well as deaths so that future mistakes made can be avoided and not cause actual deaths in the future.

The student wants to point out an issue specific to investigations of diving accidents. Which option MOST effectively uses relevant information from the notes to accomplish this goal?
- A) Accidents involving specialized equipment can require greater expertise to handle properly, with rebreather equipment being especially problematic for cases run by investigators who are not diving experts.
- B) There is encouragement within the diving community to report "near misses" as well as deaths so that mistakes made can be avoided and not cause actual deaths in the future.
- C) An investigation will usually follow a diving accident that was either fatal or could potentially result in litigation, as a lawsuit against any member of the diving community could affect the public's perception of the practice in general.
- D) The United States Coast Guard will often investigate a death involving a dive from a vessel in coastal waters.

23. *A scholar of the highest type and a fearless defender of true and honest thinking, Huxley certainly was: but the quality which gives meaning to his work, which makes it live, is a certain human quality due to the fact that Huxley was always keenly alive to the relation of science to the problems of life. _____, he was not content with the mere acquirement of knowledge; and for this reason, also, he could not quietly wait until the world should come to his way of thinking. Much of the time, therefore, which he would otherwise naturally have spent in research, he spent in contending for and in endeavoring to popularize the facts of science.*

Which option completes the text with the MOST logical transition?
   A)   However
   B)   For this reason
   C)   Even so
   D)   In conclusion

24. While researching a topic, a student has taken the following notes:
   - *Hemp and linen are both fabrics made from natural plant fibers.*

   - *Linen is made from the cellulose fibers in the stalks of flax plants.*

   - *Hemp comes from fibers in the stalks of the Cannabis sativa plant.*

   - *Both fabrics are very breathable and stand up well to washing.*

   - *Hemp fabric tends to be rougher than linen but is also eight times stronger due to its fiber bundles being longer.*

The student wants to emphasize the similarities between the two fabrics. Which option MOST effectively uses relevant information from the notes to accomplish this goal?
   A)   Linen is made from the cellulose fibers in the stalks of flax plants, which is something that it has in common with hemp fabric.
   B)   Hemp fabric tends to be rougher than linen but is also eight times stronger due to its fiber bundles being longer.
   C)   Hemp and linen should be viewed as basically the same thing because both are made of cellulose fibers taken from the stalks of plants.
   D)   Both plant fibers are very breathable and stand up well to washing when woven into fabric.

25. *The latter had reason to dread that, if the Turks were not checked, Constantinople, their capital, would soon share the same fate as Jerusalem. _____, about the year 1073, the Greek Emperor, Manuel VII, sent to supplicate the assistance of the great Pope Gregory VII against the Turks. Till now there had prevailed a spirit of antagonism between the Greek and Latin churches, the former refusing to yield obedience to the pope of the West as the universal head of the Church.*

Which option completes the text with the MOST logical transition?
   A)   Accordingly
   B)   Moreover
   C)   However
   D)   Despite this

26. While researching a topic, a student has taken the following notes:

- *Observational studies are research studies in which researchers record information about subjects while avoiding manipulating the study environment.*

- *Two types of observational studies are cross-sectional studies and longitudinal studies.*

- *Cross-sectional studies focus on a single point in time to analyze data from a population.*

- *Longitudinal studies repeatedly measure individuals over prolonged periods of time.*

- *A longitudinal study is best for examining changes, while a cross-sectional study is best used to describe the current situation.*

The student wants to explain how one might choose between the two types of observational study. Which option MOST effectively uses relevant information from the notes to accomplish this goal?

A) Longitudinal studies repeatedly measure individuals over prolonged periods of time, while cross-sectional studies focus on single points in time to analyze data from a population.

B) A longitudinal study is best for examining changes, while a cross-sectional study is best used to describe a current situation.

C) Two types of observational studies are cross-sectional studies and longitudinal studies.

D) Longitudinal studies are objectively better for getting more accurate results over time.

27. While researching a topic, a student has taken the following notes:

- *John Ronald Reuel (J.R.R.) Tolkien was an English writer and philologist.*

- *He was the author of several high fantasy works set in the realm of Middle Earth, including The Hobbit and The Lord of the Rings.*

- *From 1925 to 1945, Tolkien was a Fellow of Pembroke College and the Rawlinson and Bosworth Professor of Anglo-Saxon at the University of Oxford.*

- *Still at Oxford, he was a Fellow of Merton College and the Merton Professor of English Language and Literature from 1945 to 1959, when he retired.*

- *Tolkien was close friends with fellow fantasy author C.S. Lewis.*

The student wants to focus on Tolkien's academic career. Which option MOST effectively uses relevant information from the notes to accomplish this goal?

A) English writer and philologist John Ronald Reuel (J.R.R.) Tolkien wrote many high fantasy books and worked at the University of Oxford until his retirement in 1959.

B) Tolkien and close friend C.S. Lewis were both prolific fantasy authors, but Tolkien also worked in academia, remaining at the University of Oxford until he retired in 1959.

C) Tolkien's tenure at Oxford lasted from 1925 – 1959, during which time he first held the positions of Rawlinson and Bosworth Professor of Anglo-Saxon and then Merton Professor of English Language and Literature starting in 1945.

D) Tolkien was the author of several high fantasy works set in the realm of Middle Earth, including *The Hobbit* and *The Lord of the Rings*.

1. *A year later I went to the parochial school, but did not stay long, for they would not have me. I was a(n) _____ at seven and an agnostic at eight, and I objected to the prayers every five minutes. I had no respect for ceremonies. They did not impress my imagination in the slightest, partly because I learned at an early age to see the hypocrisy of many good people.*

Which option completes the text with the MOST logical and precise word or phrase?
- A) skeptic
- B) altar boy
- C) pious child
- D) religious adherent

2. *It was an age of ferment. Nothing was settled, though much was opened—new worlds and new ideas. In science, Copernicus and Vesalius may be chosen as representative figures: they typify the new cosmology and the scientific emphasis on direct observation.*

As used in the text, what does the word *ferment* MOST nearly mean?
- A) agitation
- B) brewing
- C) rot
- D) growth

3. *What was it that enabled the Greeks, in the crucial test, the ultimate contingency, to turn back the Persians and maintain their independence? History says that it was the result of the battles of Marathon and Salamis, in which the Greeks were triumphant over the Persians. This is true only in a limited sense. The battle of Marathon, in 490 B.C., did not save Greece, for the Persians came back again more powerful than ever. At Thermopylæ, Leonidas and his band died vainly, for the hosts of Xerxes overran all Greece north of the isthmus of Corinth. They took Athens and burned the temples on the Acropolis. They were triumphant on the land.*

Which option BEST states the main purpose of the text?
- A) It explains why the Persians chose to conquer Greece.
- B) It states several theories about the same series of events.
- C) It introduces an idea that it then refutes.
- D) It states a theory that it then supports.

4. *As I looked on him, his countenance expressed the utmost extent of malice and treachery. I thought with a sensation of madness on my promise of creating another like to him, and trembling with passion, tore to pieces the thing on which I was engaged. The wretch saw me destroy the creature on whose future existence he depended for happiness, and with a howl of devilish despair and revenge, withdrew.*

Which option BEST states the function of the underlined sentence in the text as a whole?
- A) It sets up the character description in the sentences that follow.
- B) It explains who the narrator is looking at in the next sentence.
- C) It provides a description of the appearance of an important character.
- D) It sets up the reason for a decision made in the next sentence.

5. Text 1

In attempting to understand the animals, I have used a method a great deal like that of the village boy, who when questioned as to how he located the stray horse for which a reward of twenty dollars had been offered, replied, "I just thought what I would do if I were a horse and where I would go—and there I went and found him." In some such way I have tried to think why animals do certain things, I have studied them in many places and under all conditions, and those acts of theirs which, if performed by children, would come under the head of wisdom and intelligence, I have classified as such.

Text 2

My father was a St. Bernard, my mother was a collie, but I am a Presbyterian. This is what my mother told me; I do not know these nice distinctions myself. To me they are only fine large words meaning nothing. My mother had a fondness for such; she liked to say them, and see other dogs look surprised and envious, as wondering how she got so much education.

Which option MOST accurately describes the sentiments of Text 1 toward the personification of animals with respect to Text 2's approach?

- A) Text 1's author sees personification of animals as a childish practice; for Text 2's author, personification forms the basis of an entire story.
- B) Text 1's author seeks to use personification to better understand animal behavior; Text 2's author uses personification as a comedic narrative device.
- C) Text 1's author uses personification of animals in a scientific way; Text 2's author uses personification in a religious way.
- D) Text 2 does not use or discuss the personification of animals; only Text 1 does this.

6. *Her explanation was that a man had seized her on the ice, or as she left it, had dragged her across the fields, and had shut her up in a house, from which she escaped, crawled to her father's home, and, when she found herself unable to go further, tossed her hat towards the farm door.* <u>Neither such a man as she described, nor the house in which she had been imprisoned, was ever found. The girl's character was excellent, nothing pointed to her condition being the result d'une orgie échevelée; but the neighbors, of course, made insinuations, and a lady of my acquaintance, who visited the girl's mother, found herself almost alone in placing a charitable construction on the adventure.</u>

The sentences underlined suggest that which of the following is true of the girl's neighbors?

- A) They were not fooled by her obvious lie about what had happened to her.
- B) They thought that she had been kidnapped on the ice.
- C) They came to visit the girl to understand what had happened.
- D) They doubted the girl's story about what had happened.

7. *What is the size, mass, and distance of each of the planets? What satellites, like our Moon, do they possess? What are their temperatures? And those other, sporadic members of our system, comets and meteors, what are they? What are their movements? How do they originate? And the Sun itself, what is its composition, what is the source of its heat, how did it originate? Is it running down?*

Which option BEST describes the overall structure of the text?
A) It asks its reader a series of questions to answer.
B) It poses a series of general theoretical questions about planets and other heavenly bodies.
C) It poses a series of practical questions about a specific group of planets and other heavenly bodies.
D) It uses a series of questions to cast doubt upon established knowledge about planets.

8. *The graph below tracks the total number of books published by Project Gutenberg over a period of ten years. The x-axis counts the years from 1994 – 2014, and the y-axis gives the values for the total number of books. Dover believes that, in 2002, a significant cultural shift took place toward higher participation in preserving public domain works.*

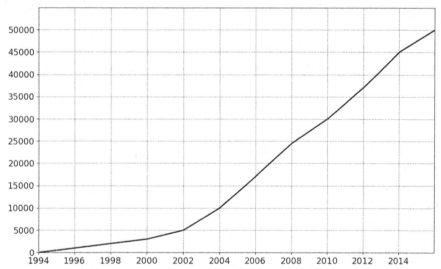

Total Number of Books Published by Project Gutenberg 1994 – 2014

Which option BEST describes data from the graph to justify Dover's conclusion?
A) The number of books published in 2008 was about 25,000, which is ten or more times the number that had been published in 2000.
B) About 2,500 books were published in 2000 as opposed to 5,000 in 2002.
C) About 5,000 books were published in 2002 as compared to about 10,000 in 2004.
D) The number of books published took eight years (from 1994 – 2002) to reach 5,000, but another 5,000 books were published in the period between 2002 and 2004.

9. *Constitutions have changed with habits of life, and the treatment of disorders has changed to meet the new conditions. New diseases have shown themselves of which Doctor Butts had no cognizance; new continents have given us plants with medicinal virtues previously unknown; new sciences, and even the mere increase of recorded experience, have added a thousand remedies to those known to the age of the Tudors. If the College of Physicians had been organized into a board of orthodoxy, and every novelty of treatment had been regarded as a crime against society, which a law had been established to punish, the hundreds who die annually from preventable causes would have been thousands and tens of thousands.*

Which option BEST states the main idea of the text?
   A)   Doctor Butts was inadequate as a physician and would have killed thousands if allowed to make his recommendations mandatory.
   B)   Medicine in the time of the Tudors was so much worse due to the College of Physicians being organized into a board of orthodoxy.
   C)   If the regulation of medical study were too stringent as new theories were being developed, important discoveries would never have been made.
   D)   If there was a stronger central authority in medicine, there would be more cures found for preventable illnesses.

10. *The point of cardinal importance in connection with Mendelism is that it does reveal a law capable of being numerically stated, and apparently applicable to a large number of isolated factors in living things. Indeed it was this attention to isolated factors which was the first and essential part of Mendel's method. For example, others had been content to look at the pea as a whole. Mendel applied his analytic method to such things as the color of the pea, _____, its dwarfness or height, and so on.*

Which option MOST logically completes the text?
   A)   the methods used to grow it
   B)   the smooth or wrinkled character of its skin
   C)   the general enjoyment of its taste
   D)   the way it was harvested

11. *A group of researchers conducted an experiment to see how the relative reduction in people's stress levels was affected by the addition of goats to their yoga practice, with the expectation that the levity provided by the goats would provide greater de-stressing benefits. The researchers recruited several participants from local yoga studios and placed them in one month of twice weekly vinyasa yoga classes without goats, followed by one month of twice weekly vinyasa yoga sessions with goats; they then interviewed the participants at the end of the second month about how the experiences compared.*

Which quotation from a participant would BEST support the researchers' hypothesis?
   A)   "I felt so free after spending an hour posing with a tiny goat climbing on top of me. You just don't get so many chances to laugh in a normal yoga class."
   B)   "The stress of the day just melts away the moment I get on the mat."
   C)   "I think the yoga is more important than the goat when it comes to the effects of the practice."
   D)   "My goat seemed more anxious than I was at the start of the class."

12. *Jane Eyre is an 1847 novel by Charlotte Brontë. Brontë portrays the character of Mr. Rochester as intriguing and witty but unkind, as evidenced by his attempt to make the titular heroine jealous in Chapter 22 by pretending that he intends to marry another woman.*

Which quotation from Jane Eyre MOST effectively illustrates the claim about Mr. Rochester?
- A) "I dreamt of Miss Ingram all the night: in a vivid morning dream I saw her closing the gates of Thornfield against me and pointing me out another road; and Mr. Rochester looked on with his arms folded—smiling sardonically, as it seemed, at both her and me."
- B) "I had heard from Mrs. Fairfax in the interim of my absence: The party at the hall was dispersed; Mr. Rochester had left for London three weeks ago, but he was then expected to return in a fortnight. Mrs. Fairfax surmised that he was gone to make arrangements for his wedding, as he had talked of purchasing a new carriage: she said the idea of his marrying Miss Ingram still seemed strange to her; but from what everybody said, and from what she had herself seen, she could no longer doubt that the event would shortly take place."
- C) "A true Janian reply! Good angels be my guard! She comes from the other world—from the abode of people who are dead; and tells me so when she meets me alone here in the gloaming! If I dared, I'd touch you, to see if you are substance or shadow, you elf!—but I'd as soon offer to take hold of a blue ignis fatuus light in a marsh. Truant! truant!" he added, when he had paused an instant. "Absent from me a whole month, and forgetting me quite, I'll be sworn!"
- D) "You must see the carriage, Jane, and tell me if you don't think it will suit Mrs. Rochester exactly; and whether she won't look like Queen Boadicea, leaning back against those purple cushions. I wish, Jane, I were a trifle better adapted to match with her externally. Tell me now, fairy as you are—can't you give me a charm, or a philter, or something of that sort, to make me a handsome man?"

13. *The Essay on Criticism is, however, more than an example of the interrelation of literature and politics in the eighteenth century; and it is more than a step on the way to its author's immortalizing in lead. It presents, albeit not very imaginatively, a statement of many of the literary theories and attitudes of the Augustan period. However brief and incomplete, the remarks about the language of poetry and upon the effects of certain literary passages are _____.*

Which option MOST logically completes the text?
- A) uncreative and lazy attempts to exercise a type of practical criticism
- B) of interest as imperfect exercises in a type of practical criticism
- C) the least interesting possible use of the period's literary theories
- D) nothing that presents any value for study

14. *Not so is it with a second foreign element, which silently dropped into the soil of Universities, like the grain of mustard seed in the parable; and, like that grain, grew into a tree, in whose branches a whole aviary of fowls took shelter. That element is the element of Endowment. It differed from the preceding, in ___ original design to serve as a prop to the young plant, not to be a parasite upon it.*

Which option completes the text so that it conforms to the conventions of Standard English?
- A) its
- B) it's
- C) their
- D) there

15. *Ritter discovered the extension of the spectrum into the invisible region beyond the violet; and, in recent times, this ultra-violet emission has had peculiar interest conferred upon it by the admirable research of Professor Stokes. The complete spectrum of the sun consists, therefore, of three distinct parts: first, of ultra-red rays of high heating power, but unsuited to the purposes of _____ of luminous rays which display the succession of colors, red, orange, yellow, green, blue, indigo, violet; thirdly, of ultra-violet rays which, like the ultra-red ones, are incompetent to excite vision, but which, unlike the ultra-red rays, possess a very feeble heating power.*

Which option completes the text so that it conforms to the conventions of Standard English?
- A) vision, secondly,
- B) vision, secondly;
- C) vision; secondly,
- D) vision, secondly

16. *In which category are we to place the letters of Keats, including those that have been very recently unearthed by diligent literary _____ poetry is so exquisite, so radiant with imaginative color, that to see such a man in the light of common day, among the ordinary cares and circumstances of the lower world, is necessarily a descent and a disillusion.*

Which option completes the text so that it conforms to the conventions of Standard English?
- A) excavation: His
- B) excavation? His
- C) excavation. His
- D) excavation; his

17. *Filled with this idea, and animated by that pure zeal for science, which is its own best reward, _____. But for the considerations I have ventured to suggest, such a resolution on the part of such a man would be surely calculated to excite regret.*

Which option completes the text so that it conforms to the conventions of Standard English?
- A) the Sanskrit tongue becomes Schlegel's subject of study
- B) the study of the Sanskrit tongue inspires Schlegel
- C) the Sanskrit tongue moves Schlegel to study
- D) Schlegel resolves to betake him to the study of the Sanskrit tongue

18. *Jeanne sang more than she danced, and though she carried garlands like the other boys and girls, and hung them on the boughs of the Fairies' Tree, she _____ into the parish church, and lay them on the altars of St. Margaret and St. Catherine. It was said among the villagers that Jeanne's godmother had once seen the fairies dancing; but though some of the older people believed in the Good Ladies, it does not seem that Jeanne and the other children had faith in them or thought much about them.*

Which option completes the text so that it conforms to the conventions of Standard English?
- A) liked better, to take the flowers
- B) liked, better, to take the flowers
- C) liked better to take the flowers
- D) liked better: to take the flowers

19. *Ambroise Paré was born in the village of Bourg-Hersent, near Laval, in Maine, France, about 1510. He was trained as a barber-surgeon at a time when a barber-surgeon was inferior to a surgeon and the professions of surgeon and physician were kept apart by the law of the Church that forbade a physician to shed blood. Under ___ he served his apprenticeship is unknown, but by 1533 he was in Paris, where he received an appointment as house surgeon at the Hotel Dieu.*

Which option completes the text so that it conforms to the conventions of Standard English?
   A)   what
   B)   who
   C)   which
   D)   whom

20. *A miracle alone could have made Baxter a poet; the cold, clear light of reason "paled the ineffectual fires" of his imagination; all things presented themselves to his vision "with hard outlines, colorless, and with no surrounding atmosphere." That he did, _____, write verses, so creditable as to justify a judicious modern critic in their citation and approval, can perhaps be accounted for only as one of the phenomena of that subtle and transforming influence to which even his stern nature was unconsciously yielding. Baxter was in love.*

Which option completes the text with the MOST logical transition?
   A)   because of this
   B)   nevertheless
   C)   consequently
   D)   for this reason

21. *All we know is the fact that this planet moves in a certain order, and at a fixed rate, and that the speed is of itself sufficient to rend the hardest rocks; yet the delicate down which rests so lightly upon the flower is undisturbed. It is, _____, evident that matter is endued with powers, by which mass is bound to mass, and atom to atom; these powers are not the results of any of the motions which we have examined, but, acting in antagonism to them, they sustain our globe in its present form.*

Which option completes the text with the MOST logical transition?
   A)   therefore
   B)   initially
   C)   by comparison
   D)   by contrast

22. While researching a topic, a student has taken the following notes:
   • *The dugong and three species of manatee are the four living species of the order Sirenia.*

   • *Neither dugongs nor manatees have hind limbs or dorsal fins.*

   • *Manatees have paddle-shaped tails, while dugongs have whale-like, fluked tails.*

   • *Manatees usually feed at or near the water's surface and have short snouts.*

   • *Dugongs have longer, trunk-like snouts and eat seagrasses from the sea floor.*

The student wants to emphasize the differences between manatees and dugongs. Which option MOST effectively uses relevant information from the notes to accomplish this goal?

A) Dugongs and manatees are more different than similar, as evidenced by the dugong's longer, trunk-like snout.

B) Though they have different snout and tail shapes, dugongs and manatees are both part of the order Sirenia.

C) Neither creature has hind limbs or dorsal fins, and both are part of the order Sirenia, though only dugongs have long, trunk-like snouts to feed on seagrasses.

D) While manatees usually feed at or near the water's surface with their short snouts, dugongs swim along the bottom of their habitat and eat seagrasses using longer, trunk-like snouts.

23. *History also tells us that the field of the supernatural has rewarded its cultivators with a harvest, perhaps not less luxuriant, but of a different character. It has produced an almost infinite diversity of Religions. These, if we set aside the ethical concomitants upon which natural knowledge also has a claim, are composed of information about Supernature; they tell us of the attributes of supernatural beings, of their relations with Nature, and of the operations by which their interference with the ordinary course of events can be secured or averted. It does not appear, _____, that supernaturalists have attained to any agreement about these matters, or that history indicates a widening of the influence of supernaturalism on practice, with the onward flow of time.*

Which option completes the text with the MOST logical transition?

A) therefore

B) however

C) in consequence

D) as a result

24. While researching a topic, a student has taken the following notes:

- *Robin McKinley is an American author known for writing fantasy novels and fairytale retellings.*

- *Her 1984 novel The Hero and the Crown won the Newbery Medal for best new American children's book.*

- *In 2022, she was named the 39th Damon Knight Memorial Grand Master by the Science Fiction and Fantasy Writers Association.*

- *Her fairytale retellings often have a "feminist twist."*

- *McKinley has stated that she has strong feelings about the need for heroines in stories to be "doing things," and she sees the general selection of fantasy literature with female leads as scarce and unsatisfactory.*

The student wants to emphasize McKinley's feminism in her fairytale retellings. Which option MOST effectively uses relevant information from the notes to accomplish this goal?

A) The "feminist twist" in most of McKinley's fairytale retellings stems from her desire to show more fantasy heroines "doing things," not simply serving as the love interests of male leads.

B) Robin McKinley, 1984 winner of the Newberry Medal and 39th Damon Knight Memorial Grand Master, often writes fairytale retellings with a "feminist twist."

C) Robin McKinley won the Newberry Medal in 1984 and was named 39th Damon Knight Memorial Grand Master for her feminist fairytale retellings.

D) McKinley feels that not enough heroines in fantasy literature are shown "doing things."

25. *On his father's side he was an English country squire, but foreign residence and the Neapolitan Court had largely affected the family, in addition to that flavor of cosmopolitan culture which belongs to the more highly placed Englishmen of the Roman Communion. On his mother's side he was a member of one of the oldest and greatest families in Germany, which was only not princely. The Dalbergs, _____, had intermarried with an Italian family, the Brignoli.*

Which option completes the text with the MOST logical transition?
   A)   as a result
   B)   in consequence
   C)   however
   D)   moreover

26. While researching a topic, a student has taken the following notes:
   •   *George Washington Carver was an American agricultural scientist and inventor.*

   •   *He promoted farming methods that prevented soil depletion from repeated cotton plantings.*

   •   *He also promoted alternative crops to cotton, including peanuts and sweet potatoes, which farmers could use as food sources.*

   •   *He was among the most prominent Black scientists of the early 1900s.*

   •   *He came up with more than 300 uses of peanuts to encourage people to plant them.*

The student wants to encourage their peers to view George Washington Carver as more than "that peanut guy." Which option MOST effectively uses relevant information from the notes to accomplish this goal?
   A)   George Washington Carver came up with more than 300 uses of peanuts to encourage people to plant them instead of cotton on their farms.
   B)   American agricultural scientist and inventor George Washington Carver came up with more than 300 uses of peanuts and promoted farming methods that prevented soil depletion from repeated cotton plantings.
   C)   Carver's work in preventing soil depletion from repeated cotton plantings also extended to promoting alternative crops, such as peanuts and sweet potatoes, that farmers could use as food sources.
   D)   Although he is currently known best for identifying more than 300 uses of peanuts, George Washington Carver was among the most prominent Black scientists of the early 1900s.

27. While researching a topic, a student has taken the following notes:
   •   *John Lopez is an American sculptor who makes life-size hybrid metal sculptures using discarded farm equipment and bronze.*

   •   *He made 12 life-size presidential monuments for display in The City of Presidents attraction in Rapid City, South Dakota.*

   •   *The presidents Lopez sculpted include Presidents Kennedy, Carter, Grant, and Garfield.*

   •   *He made a life-size metal buffalo called Dakotah, which is on display at the Dakotah Steak House and Restaurant.*

   •   *He lives in South Dakota.*

The student wants to emphasize Lopez's connection to the state of South Dakota. Which option MOST effectively uses relevant information from the notes to accomplish this goal?

A) Located in South Dakota, John Lopez is an American sculptor who makes life-size hybrid metal sculptures using discarded farm equipment and bronze.

B) South Dakota artist John Lopez has made hybrid metal sculptures of subjects ranging from American presidents to life-size metal Buffalos.

C) From making twelve sculptures for the City of Presidents in Rapid City to building a life-size metal buffalo for the Dakotah Steak House and Restaurant, John Lopez has thoroughly left his mark on his home state of South Dakota.

D) John Lopez has proven himself particularly adept at making hybrid metal sculptures during his time in South Dakota.

Practice Test #1
Math

For questions 1 – 16, work the problem and choose the most correct answer. For questions 17 – 22, work the problem and enter the correct answer in the space provided. You may use a calculator, but remember: some questions may be more efficiently answered through reasoning rather than the use of a calculator.

Module I

1. What is the axis of symmetry for the given parabola?

$$y = -2(x + 3)^2 + 5$$

A) $y = 3$
B) $x = -3$
C) $y = -3$
D) $x = 3$

2. Which of the following is equivalent to $z^3(z + 2)^2 - 4z^3 + 2$?
A) 2
B) $z^5 + 4z^4 + 4z^3 + 2$
C) $z^6 + 4z^3 + 2$
D) $z^5 + 4z^4 + 2$

3. Which of the following is an equation of the line that passes through the points $(4, -3)$ and $(-2, 9)$ in the xy-plane?
A) $y = -2x + 5$
B) $y = -\frac{1}{2}x - 1$
C) $y = \frac{1}{2}x - 5$
D) $y = 2x - 11$

4. What is the domain of the inequality $\left|\frac{x}{8}\right| \geq 1$?
A) $(-\infty, \infty)$
B) $[8, \infty)$
C) $(-\infty, -8]$
D) $(-\infty, -8] \cup [8, \infty)$

5. In the xy-plane, the line given by which of the following equations is parallel to the line $3x + 2y = 10$?

  A) $y = -3x + 2$

  B) $y = -\frac{3}{2}x - 10$

  C) $y = \frac{1}{3}x + 5$

  D) $y = \frac{2}{3}x - 10$

6. Which of the following represents a linear equation?

  A) $\sqrt[3]{y} = x$

  B) $\sqrt[3]{x} = y$

  C) $\sqrt[3]{y} = x^2$

  D) $y = \sqrt[3]{x^3}$

7. Justin has a summer lawn care business and earns \$40 for each lawn he mows. He also pays \$35 per week in business expenses. Which of the following expressions represents Justin's profit after x weeks if he mows m number of lawns?

  A) $40m - 35x$
  B) $40m + 35x$
  C) $35x(40 + m)$
  D) $35(40m + x)$

8. What are the real zero(s) of the following polynomial?
$$2n^2 + 2n - 12 = 0$$

  A) $\{2\}$
  B) $\{-3, 2\}$
  C) $\{2, 4\}$
  D) There are no real zeros of n.

9. Which graph shows the solution to $y = 2x + 1$?

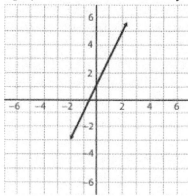

A)

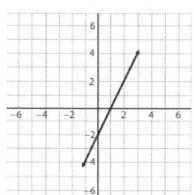

B)

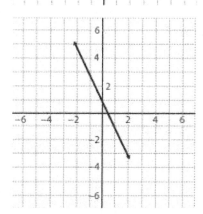

C)

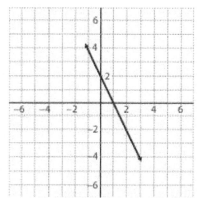

D)

10. A cube with volume 27 cubic meters is inscribed within a sphere such that all of the cube's vertices touch the sphere. What is the length of the sphere's radius?

    A)   2.6 meters
    B)   3 meters
    C)   5.2 meters
    D)   9 meters

11. Find the value of x in the triangle below.

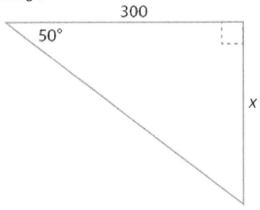

    A) $300(\sin 50°)$
    B) $300(\cos 50°)$
    C) $300(\tan 50°)$
    D) $300(\csc 50°)$

12. What is the domain of the piecewise function shown in the graph?

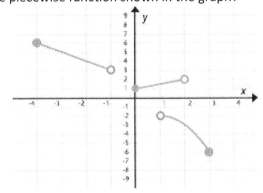

    A) $D: (-4, -1) \cup (0, 3)$
    B) $D: (-4, 3)$
    C) $D: (-4, 1) \cup (0, 3)$
    D) $D: (-4, -1) \cup (0, 1) \cup (1, 3)$

13. Which of the following defines y as a function of x?

I. $y^2 + x = 3$

II.

x	y
0	4
1	5
2	8
3	13
4	20

III. $y = \sin(\theta)$

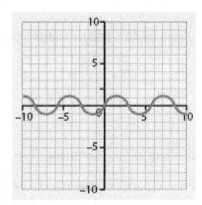

A) II only
B) I and II only
C) II and III only
D) I, II, III only

14. Which of the following is the vertical asymptote of the given function?
$$f(x) = \frac{x + 4}{-2x - 6}$$

A) $y = \frac{1}{2}$
B) $y = -2$
C) $x = 3$
D) $x = -3$

15. What is the slope of the graph below?

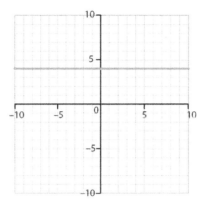

    A)   −5
    B)   0
    C)   −4
    D)   4

16. If the length of a rectangle is increased by 40% and its width is decreased by 40%, what is the effect on the rectangle's area?
    A.   It increases by 20%.
    B.   It increases by 16%.
    C.   There is no increase or decrease.
    D.   It decreases by 16%.

For questions 17 – 22, work the problem and enter your answer in the space provided.

17. The formula for distance is $d = v \times t$, where v is the object's velocity and t is the time. How long will it take a plane to fly 4,000 miles from Chicago to London if the plane flies at a constant rate of 500 mph?

18. A grocery store sold 30% of its pears and had 455 pears remaining. How many pears did the grocery store start with?

19. A bassist practicing for his latest gig can learn songs at a constant rate of 2 measures per minute. At what rate, in measures per hour, does the bassist learn songs?

20. Monty spent $87 on pizza and wings for a party. Each pizza cost $12 and each serving of wings cost $9. If Monty bought 5 pizzas, how many servings of wings did he buy?

21. The function q is defined by $q(x) = x^3 + 125$. What is the value of $q(x)$ when $x = 4$?

22. The perimeter of an equilateral triangle is 96 inches. The height of this triangle is $n\sqrt{3}$ inches, where n is a constant. What is the value of n?

Module II

For questions 1 – 16, work the problem and choose the most correct answer. For questions 17 – 22, work the problem and enter the correct answer in the space provided. You may use a calculator, but remember: some questions may be more efficiently answered through reasoning rather than the use of a calculator.

1. If a student answers 42 out of 48 questions correctly on a quiz, what percentage of questions did she answer correctly?
   A) 82.5%
   B) 85%
   C) 87.5%
   D) 90%

2. The population of a town was 7,250 in 2014 and 7,375 in 2015. What was the percent increase from 2014 to 2015 to the nearest tenth of a percent?
   A) 1.5%
   B) 1.6%
   C) 1.7%
   D) 1.8%

3. Which of the following is a solution to the inequality $2x + y \leq -10$?
   A) $(0, 0)$
   B) $(10, 2)$
   C) $(10, 10)$
   D) $(-10, -10)$

4. What are the roots of the equation $y = 16 \times 3 - 48 \times 2$?
   A) $\left\{ \frac{(3+i\sqrt{5})}{2}, \frac{3-i\sqrt{5}}{2} \right\}$
   B) $\{0, 3, -3\}$
   C) $\{0, 3i, -3i\}$
   D) $\{0, 3\}$

5. Bryce has 34 coins worth a total of $6.25. If all the coins are dimes or quarters, how many of EACH coin does Bryce have?
   A) 9 dimes and 15 quarters
   B) 10 dimes and 24 quarters
   C) 15 dimes and 19 quarters
   D) 19 dimes and 15 quarters

6. An ice chest contains 24 sodas, some regular and some diet. The ratio of diet soda to regular soda is 1:3. How many regular sodas are there in the ice chest?
   A) 1
   B) 4
   C) 18
   D) 24

7. In the circle below with center O, the minor arc ACB measures 5 feet. What is the measurement of $m \angle AOB$?

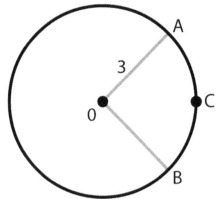

- A) 90
- B) 90.5
- C) 95
- D) 95.5

8. In the fall, 425 students pass the math benchmark. In the spring, 680 students pass the same benchmark. What is the percentage increase in passing scores from fall to spring?
- A) 37.5%
- B) 55%
- C) 60%
- D) 62.5%

9. A baby weighed 7.5 pounds at birth and gained weight at a rate of 6 ounces per month for the first six months. Which equation describes the baby's weight in ounces, y, after t months?
- A) $y = 6t + 7.5$
- B) $y = 6t + 120$
- C) $y = 7.5t + 120$
- D) $y = 6t + 7.5$

10. A fruit stand sells apples, bananas, and oranges at a ratio of 3:2:1. If the fruit stand sells 20 bananas, how many total pieces of fruit does the fruit stand sell?
- A) 10
- B) 30
- C) 40
- D) 60

11. The given equation represents which type of conic section?
$$x2 + 2xy + 4y2 + 6x + 14y = 86$$

- A) circle
- B) ellipse
- C) hyperbola
- D) parabola

12. A person earning a salary between $75,000 and $100,000 per year will pay $10,620 in taxes plus 20% of any amount over $75,000. What would a person earning $80,000 per year pay in taxes?
   A) $10,620
   B) $11,620
   C) $12,120
   D) $12,744

13. A square-based pyramid has a height of 10 cm. If the length of the side of the square is 6 cm, what is the surface area of the pyramid?
   A) 36 cm
   B) $3\sqrt{109}$ cm
   C) 100 cm
   D) 161.3 cm^2

14. A bike store is having a 30% off sale, and one of the bikes is on sale for $385. What was the original price of this bike?
   A) $253.00
   B) $450.00
   C) $500.50
   D) $550.00

15. Tiles are $12.51 per square yard. What will it cost to cover the floor of a room with tiles if the room is 10 feet wide and 12 feet long?
   A) $166.80
   B) $178.70
   C) $184.60
   D) $190.90

16. Jane earns $15 per hour babysitting. If she starts with $275 in her bank account, which equation represents how many hours (h) she will have to babysit for her account to reach $400?
   A) $400 = 275 + 15h$

   B) $400 = 15h$

   C) $400 = \frac{15}{h} + 275$

   D) $400 = -275 - 15h$

For questions 17 – 22, work the problem and enter your answer in the space provided.

17. The graph below shows Company X's profits for the years 2010 to 2013. How much more profit did Company X make in 2013 than in 2012?

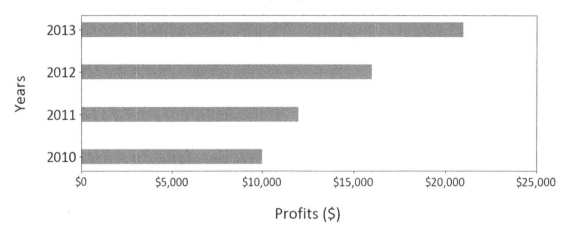

18. In 2016, LeBron James averaged 26.4 points per game over 74 games. How many points did James score that year? (Round to the nearest whole number.)

19. Kim and Chris are writing a book together. Kim wrote twice as many pages as Chris, and together they wrote 240 pages. How many pages did Chris write?

20. The circle and hexagon below both share center point T. The hexagon is entirely inscribed in the circle. The circle's radius is 5. What is the area of the shaded portion?

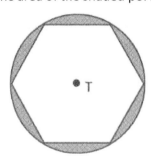

21. The graph below shows the change in temperature from 12:00 p.m. to 6:00 p.m. At what time does the temperature begin to change the most?

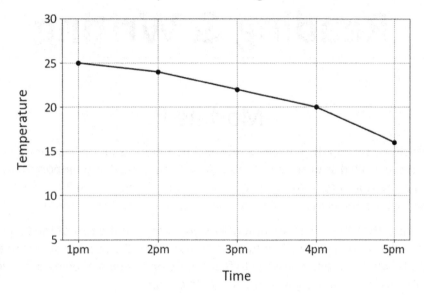

Temperature Change Over Time

22. Fifty shares of a financial stock and 10 shares of an auto stock are valued at $1,300. If 10 shares of the financial stock and 10 shares of the auto stock are valued at $500, what is the value of 50 shares of the auto stock?

Answer Key #1
Reading & Writing

Module I

1. C: Option C effectively sets up the passage's subsequent emphasis on the lack of value of utterances of these men, as those viewed as unskilled are also likely to be viewed as unimportant. Options A and D attempt to assign a physical state to the people being described, and option B assigns these people an emotional state; however, the passage only discusses how Demetrius views them.

2. A: Option A aligns with the emphasis on practicality and morals in the rest of the first sentence. Option B suggests a desire for a more adventurous approach than the passage seems to advocate for, and options C and D both require the passage to focus more on the idea of being perceived as smart than the practical concerns of how a government should be run.

3. D: Option D best describes the comparisons made throughout the sonnet, which are not maliciously unflattering as in option C (as evidenced by the loving final couplet), but do deliberately and explicitly avoid flattering the subject, which rules out option A. Option B would require the sonnet to give descriptions of this ideal woman, but instead it points out that its subject is not the ideal.

4. A: Option A correctly notes that this sentence clarifies the protagonist's (i.e., the cat's) motivation; the cat believes that nobody cares what becomes of it, so it decides to give up, lay down in the corner, and sleep. Option B is incorrect because it does not elaborate on any previously expressed ideas, nor does it provide any counterpoints as required for option D. Since the entire passage is presented in first-person perspective, option C's assertion that only this sentence provides insight into the protagonist's mind is incorrect.

5. B: Option B expresses Tolstoy's negative view toward property ownership as evidenced by his approval of Proudhon's statement that "property is theft." Options A, C, and D argue against a lack of respect for landowners, which does not fit with this view of property.

6. B: Option B reflects the information in the passage as it relates to how the plants best absorb nitrogen. The passage explicitly states that plants cannot adequately take in nitrogen from the atmosphere, which rules out option A. The passage does not suggest any support for the idea of changing the plants themselves, as offered in option C; instead, it emphasizes nitrogenous compounds in the soil. Option D presents a similar issue as option C.

7. C: Option C correctly identifies the passage as being about the unsuccessful line laid across the channel. Option A would require the passage to state a general belief on public opinion rather than simply point out the way people felt about innovative science at the time. Option D would require the text to state an opinion on the powers the public ought to have. In order for option B to be correct, the passage would need to explain failures in galvanic current experiments.

8. D: Option D elaborates on the sentence's statement about preserving tradition in a way that fits with the question about whether fault really lies with the younger generation if standards for poetry are low.

Options A and C both declare—with varying degrees of directness—that criticism should not involve critique, which makes no sense. Option B's fear of ruffling feathers is not reflected anywhere in the text.

9. C: Option C explains how Mrs. Bennet decides that keeping Jane near potential suitor Mr. Bingley at Netherfield is more important than Jane recovering from her cold. Mrs. Bennet is only aware of (and taking credit for) the rain in option A, and option B details Mrs. Bennet receiving the note that informs her of Jane's illness and departing for Netherfield with her two youngest daughters to check on her eldest. Option D shows Mrs. Bennet advocating very strongly for Jane to be seen as desirable, but it is not her reaction to being told that Jane is sick.

10. A: Participant 7 gave the highest comfort rating, making option A the best choice. Options B and C treat the numbers assigned to participants as numbers *of* participants. Option D wrongly states that participant 18 expressed the most discomfort, when the lowest rating actually came from Participant 3.

11. A: Option A correctly observes the narrator's "old characteristic irritability" at having his thoughts interrupted. Option B would only be correct if the narrator had noted that he was doing something important, but this is not found in the passage. Options C and D state that the narrator does not want to speak with his sister and would rather speak to someone else respectively, neither of which are implied by the passage.

12. C: Option C most clearly shows that the haunt performers enjoy providing a fun experience for visitors, which is directly opposed to enjoying causing others distress. Options A and B could just as easily have been said by a person who does enjoy others' distress as by someone who does not, and option D does not relate to enjoyment of any aspect of visitors' reactions.

13. B: Option B is the best fit for the statement in the second sentence—that the problem with the litter was that it might break down and allow Dauger to be seen. Option A requires an assumption that the public will interfere with Dauger's incarceration if he is seen, which is not indicated by the text. As Dauger is the prisoner, options C and D are both incorrect.

14. B: Option B correctly uses the possessive *their*. Option A uses the place signifier *there*; Option C refers to the contraction of *they are*; and Option D uses the article *the*, which does not perform any needed function in this sentence.

15. A: Option A makes this sentence structure parallel through the use of the word *of* for both parts of this comparison. Options B, C, and D all fail to include this parallelism, with options C and D also changing the meaning of the statement by saying that the character is talking for—and to—the school, respectively.

16. C: Option C properly uses a comma to separate the introductory phrase from what comes after it. Option A omits needed punctuation, Option B's use of a colon would require the sentence to elaborate on the introductory phrase, and Option D's semicolon is incorrect because the introductory phrase does not form a complete sentence on its own.

17. D: Unlike options A, B, and C, option D does not wrongly set off the essential element of the yellow fever patients from the rest of the sentence.

18. B: Option B continues the use of the present tense established by the previous sentence. Options A and C incorrectly lapse into past tense, and option D switches to future tense.

19. C: Option C uses the pronoun *their*, which matches the plural antecedent of the Gauls. Option A would be the proper pronoun for a singular woman, while Option B would be the pronoun used for a singular man. Option D uses *its*, which should be used for objects, not a group of people.

20. C: Option C recognizes that England's inability to defend its entire empire with its army alone was the reason for which it created subsidiary armies. Option A would mean that the second sentence provides additional information that is not a continuation of what is said in the first sentence. Options B and D implies that creating subsidiary armies is not an expected outcome of this realization.

21. D: Option D reflects the difference between the dead and living proteins indicated by the word *instead* at the start of the sentence. Options A, B, and C do not indicate contradictions.

22. A: Option A points out the specific issue of finding investigators who understand the complex equipment involved, such as rebreather equipment. Options B and D share facts from the notes that do not point out any diving investigation-specific issue. Option C makes an unfounded claim about the effects of an isolated lawsuit on the diving community as a whole and does not point out any issues unique to these investigations.

23. B: Option B reflects that Huxley did this because of what he felt gave meaning to his work. Options A and C demand a contradiction that the passage does not contain, and option D would require this sentence to be a conclusion to the idea being discussed, rather than part of an explanation of the topic.

24. D: Option D includes all of the similarities listed in the notes. Option A states that hemp fabric is also made from flax fibers, which is inaccurate. Option B focuses on the differences rather than similarities between the two fabrics. Option C makes an unnecessary argument for viewing the two as the same rather than merely similar.

25. A: Option A recognizes that the fear of what would happen to Constantinople is the reason that Manuel VII sent for assistance. Option B would require the second sentence to provide additional information that is not a continuation of what is said in the first sentence. Options C and D would mean that Manuel VII had done this even though it did not logically follow, which it did.

26. B: Option B explains when one would want to use each type of observational study. Option A defines the two types of observational studies but does not share when each should be used. Option C only states that the two observational study types exist. Option D arbitrarily declares one of the observational study designs the best without giving a reason for this.

27. C: Option C specifically discusses the positions that Tolkien held during his academic career. Options A and B both mention Tolkien's academic career but split the focus with other facts about his life and work. Option D only speaks of Tolkien's writing.

Module II

1. A: Since a skeptic is someone who has doubts, option A best matches the discussion in the rest of the passage about the narrator's lack of patience or respect for religious ceremony. Options B, C, and D all describe someone who shows devotion to religion.

2. A: Option A is the best match for the passage's description of a time in which "nothing was settled." Options B and C may fit for similar physical processes to fermentation in foods or beverages, but the passage does not reference either. Option D likewise is something that may occur in the physical process of fermentation but is not apt for the description of social ferment.

3. C: Option C correctly describes how the passage shares that the reigning theory is that these battles turned the tide for Greece before refuting that theory with the fact that these were not entirely successful for the Greeks. The passage does not ascribe motives to the Persians as required for Option A to be correct, and it neither states several theories, as in Option B, nor supports a stated theory, as in Option D.

4. D: Option D is correct in noting that this sentence describes the character as malicious, setting up the narrator's horror at the idea of creating another like him. The character's appearance is not described in the passage, making options A and C incorrect, and the sentence does not explain who the character is (option D).

5. B: Option B is correct. Text 1's author considers certain animal decisions as if they were made by human children, and Text 2 tells a joke from the perspective of a St. Bernard-border collie mix. Option A would require Text 1 to describe the practice of personification as childish rather than merely noting that a child had done it. Option C would require a religious reason for the personification of the canine narrator of Text 2, and option D would require said canine narrator to not exist.

6. D: Option D accurately describes the neighbors' doubts as to the truthfulness of the girl's story, which they "made insinuations" about. Option A states its own opinion on whether the girl is telling the truth; however, the passage does not state such an opinion. Option B would only be correct if the neighbors all believe the girl. For Option C to be correct, all the neighbors would have to have visited her the way the narrator's acquaintance did.

7. C: Option C is correct in identifying these questions as being about the mass and composition of a specific group of planets and heavenly bodies. For Option A to be correct, the passage would need to indicate that it expects the reader to answer these questions. Option B would require the questions to be less specific to these planets and their physical qualities. Option D would require the questions to be of a theoretical nature and challenge the status quo, while they are simply asking about physical qualities of these planets.

8. D: Option D best uses information from the graph to show that the rate of growth post-2002 is substantially higher than that of years prior. Option A makes it clear that the number of published books has risen over the years, but it does not describe how this changed after 2002. Option B only refers to a span of two years, ending in 2002. Option C only gives two figures for pre- and post-2002 and provides no information as to the relative rate of growth before and after.

9. C: Option C best states the idea behind the passage's discussion of new medical discoveries curing diseases of which Dr. Butts was never even aware. Option A states a negative opinion of Dr. Butts as a physician, of which we have no indication in the passage. Option B says that the College of Physicians was organized into a board of orthodoxy, but this was only offered as a hypothetical in the passage.

Option D contradicts the opinion stated in the passage related to the formation of orthodoxy in medicine.

10. B: Option B fits best with the rest of the list of physical characteristics of the pea. Options A and D refer to things that people do to the peas being studied rather than characteristics of the peas. Option C concerns how people feel about peas rather than any visible traits of peas.

11. A: Option A describes a participant who says she felt better after doing yoga with the goat than without the goat; this best fits the researchers' hypothesis. The participant in option B states that yoga itself helps with stress but, the participant does not compare the classes. Option C states that the goats are unimportant in terms of yoga's benefits, which is contrary to the researchers' hypothesis. Option D concerns the state of mind of one goat and is therefore irrelevant to the researchers' hypothesis.

12. D: Option D shows Mr. Rochester goading Jane by asking her to make him more handsome for his supposed intended. Options A and B are about Jane's thoughts on the lady and Mrs. Fairfax's opinion of the idea of the marriage, respectively. In option C, Mr. Rochester teases Jane, but not about the idea of him marrying someone else.

13. B: Option B makes the most sense with how the passage speaks of the Essay on Criticism as more than it appears and, though not imaginative, still useful and valuable. Options A, C, and D all present a negative view of the essay that the passage does not support.

14. A: Option A uses the correct possessive pronoun for the singular concept of the endowment. Option B is a contraction of "it is" and would not fit in the sentence. Option C would require the concept of the endowment to be plural, and option D signifies a place, not a possession.

15. C: Option C both properly separates the explanations of spectra of light in the list with a semicolon and uses a comma for separation within one part of the list. Option A uses only a comma to separate definitions in the list, which is inadequate. Option B also uses a comma for this but divides the word *secondly* from what comes after it too strongly by using a semicolon. Option D uses only a comma to separate the definitions and fails to set apart the word *secondly* at all.

16. B: Option B is correct because it acknowledges that the sentence is phrased as a question and needs to end with the word *excavation*. Options A, C, and D fail to properly punctuate the question; in particular, option D combines two sentences that make little sense being combined.

17. D: The phrase "animated by that pure zeal for science" modifies the man, Schlegel, experiencing said zeal; therefore option D is correct. With only the nonessential phrase "which is its own best reward" in between, the phrase modifying Schlegel is functionally placed just before his name. In options A, B, and C, the phrase appears to modify a different noun (the Sanskrit tongue or the study of it), which results in a dangling modifier.

18. C: Option C is correct because no punctuation is needed. Options A, B, and D all add unnecessary punctuation.

19. D: Option D uses the proper word for the person being referenced. Using the word *what*, as in option A, would be correct when referring to an object, not a person. Option B's word *who* would need to be a subject, not an object, in its clause. Option C, like option A, would require the person being referenced to be an object or title.

20. B: Option B fits best with the passage by stating that only a miracle could have led the cold, reason-driven Baxter to write poetry. Options A, C, and D would only make sense if Baxter became a poet because he was driven by reason and not, as the last sentence of the passage states, because he was in love.

21. A: Option A reflects that the first sentence provides the reasoning for the conclusion drawn by the second sentence. Option B would suggest that the statement in the second sentence is only true at first, which is not indicated in the passage. Options C and D require a comparison to be made and a contrast to be drawn, respectively, and no such differences are shown in the text.

22. D: Option D uses only notes about the species' differences to describe their eating habits. Option A only states a fact about dugongs and does not explain how this feature presents differently in manatees. Options B and C place more emphasis on the species' similarities than their differences.

23. B: Option B recognizes that this sentence makes a statement that alters readers' perceptions of what came before: this is what these supernaturalists explain, but they do not seem to agree with each other about much of it. Options A, C, and D all require this sentence to state something that logically follows because of the previous information.

24. A: Option A combines the notes on McKinley's feminism and her fairytale retellings to explain that she writes these stories because of her views on the general selection of fantasy heroines. Options B and C simply mention that she writes these feminist retellings while emphasizing the awards she has won, with option C incorrectly stating that these were both for fairytale retellings. Option D gives no indication that she writes fairytale retellings at all.

25. D: Option D reflects that this is additional information being given about the Dalbergs. Options A and B would mean that the Dalbergs intermarried with the Brignoli family because of what the sentence before said about the subject's genealogy. Option C would require them doing this to contradict the facts given in the previous sentence.

26. C: Option C places the most emphasis on Carver's work to prevent soil depletion, only listing peanuts as one of the crops that he encouraged farmers to plant. Options A, B, and C all emphasize the 300 uses of peanuts, with option C initially seeming like it will share something more worthwhile but then only referring to Carver as a prominent agricultural scientist.

27. C: Option C emphasizes the sculptures specifically stated to be on display in South Dakota and notes that this is the sculptor's home state. Options A, B, and C only refer to Lopez as being from South Dakota or spending time there, without placing enough emphasis on how much of his work is on display in his home state.

Answer Key #1
Math

Module I

1. B: The axis of symmetry will be a vertical line that runs through the vertex, which is the point $(-3, 5)$. The line of symmetry is $x = -3$.

2. D: Simplify using the order of operations—PEMDAS (parentheses, exponents, multiplication/division, addition/subtraction):

$$z^3(z + 2)^2 - 4z^3 + 2$$
$$z^3(z^2 + 4z + 4) - 4z^3 + 2$$
$$z^5 + 4z^4 + 4z^3 - 4z^3 + 2$$
$$z^5 + 4z^4 + 2$$

3. A: Use the points to find the slope:

$$m = \frac{y_2 - y_1}{x_2 - x_1} = \frac{-3 - 9}{4 - (-2)} = -2$$

Use the point-slope equation to find the equation of the line:

$$(y - y_1) = m(x - x_1)$$
$$y - (-3) = -2(x - 4)$$
$$y = -2x + 5$$

4. D: Split the absolute value inequality into two inequalities and simplify. Switch the inequality when making one side negative:

$$\frac{x}{8} \geq 1$$
$$x \geq 8$$
$$-\frac{x}{8} \geq 1$$
$$\frac{x}{8} \leq -1$$
$$x \leq -8$$
$$x \leq -8 \text{ or } x \geq 8 \rightarrow (-\infty, -8] \cup [8, \infty)$$

5. B: Find the slope of the given line. Any parallel lines will have the same slope.

$$3x + 2y = 10$$

$$2y = -3x + 10$$

$$y = -\frac{3}{2}x + 5$$

6. D: Solve each equation for y and find the equation with a power of 1.

$$\sqrt[3]{y} = x \rightarrow y = x^3$$

$$\sqrt[3]{x} = y \rightarrow y = \sqrt[3]{x}$$

$$\sqrt[3]{y} = x^2 \rightarrow y = x^6$$

$$y = \sqrt[3]{x^3} \rightarrow y = x$$

7. A: Justin's profit will be his income minus his expenses. He will earn $40 for each lawn, or 40m. He pays $35 is expenses each week, or 35w:

$$profit = 40m - 35x$$

8. B: Factor the trinomial and set each factor equal to 0.

$$2n^2 + 2n - 12 = 0$$

$$2(n^2 + n - 6) = 0$$

$$2(n + 3)(n - 2) = 0$$

$$n = -3 \text{ and } n = 2$$

9. A: The line $y = 2x + 1$ will have a slope of 2 and y-intercept of 1. The lines shown in graphs C and D have negative slopes. The line in graph B has a y-intercept of −2. Alternatively, use a table to find some coordinates, and identify the graph that contains those coordinates:

x	y
0	1
1	3
2	5

10. A: Since the cube's volume is 27, each side length is equal to $\sqrt[3]{27} = 3$. The long diagonal distance from one of the cube's vertices to its opposite vertex will provide the sphere's diameter:

$$d = \sqrt{3^2 + 3^2 + 3^2} = \sqrt{27} = 5.2$$

Half of this length is the radius, which is 2.6 meters.

11. C: Use the equation for tangent:

$$\tan 50° = \frac{x}{300}$$

$$x = 300(\tan 50°)$$

12. A: The domain is the possible values of x from left to right. Here, the domain starts at −4, inclusive, and stops at −1, exclusive. It starts again at 0, inclusive, and goes to 3, inclusive. The two line segments from 0 to 3 cross over each other, so the domain includes this whole interval. Note that closed circles represent inclusion (square brackets), and open circles represent exclusions (round brackets).

13. B: Only I and II define y as a function of x.

I. This is not a function: the equation represents a horizontal parabola, which fails the vertical line test.

II. This is a function: each x-value corresponds to only one y-value.

III. This is a function: the graph passes the vertical line test.

14. D: Find where the denominator equals 0.

$$-2x - 6 = 0$$
$$x = -3$$

15. B: The slope of a horizontal line is always 0.

16. D: The easiest way to solve this problem is to choose a specific rectangle length and width, modify them as directed, and then determine how much the area changes. The effect on the area will be the same regardless of the specific dimensions of the original rectangle. If the rectangle has sides of 100 and 10, then its area is 1,000. Increasing the length by 40% gives a new length of $(1.40)(100) = 140$. Decreasing the width by 40% gives a new width of $(0.60)(10) = 6$. The area of the modified rectangle is $(140)(6) = 840$. This eliminates answer options A, B, and C since the area clearly decreased. The change in the area is 160. The percent change in the area is the change in area (160) divided by the original area (1,000), which is 0.16, a 16% decrease.

17. Plug the given values into the equation and solve for t:

$$d = v \times t$$
$$4,000 = 500 \times t$$
$$t = \mathbf{8\ hours}$$

18. Set up an equation. If p is the original number of pears, the store has sold $0.30p$ pears. The original number minus the number sold will equal 455.

$$p - 0.30p = 455$$
$$p = \frac{455}{0.7} = \mathbf{650\ pears}$$

19. This is determined by taking the rate of measures learned per minute (2) and multiplying the value by the number of minutes in one hour (60). Thus, $2 \times 60 = \mathbf{120\ measures}$.

20. Multiply $12 by the amount of pizzas Monty ordered (5) to determine that Monty spent $60 on pizza. There is a remainder of $27 for Monty to have bought wings with. Take $27 and divide it by the cost of a serving of wings ($9) to show that Monty purchased **3 servings of wings**.

21. Insert 4 for x to determine that $4^3 = 64$. From there, add 64 to 125 $(64 + 125 = 189)$. Thus, the value of $q(x)$ when $x = \mathbf{4}$ is **189**.

22. Because the height of the equilateral triangle is $n\sqrt{3}$, the triangle can be divided into two congruent 30/60/90 right triangles. Therefore, the hypotenuse of each right triangle, because it is made up by two sides of the full triangle, is $2n$. Since the full triangle is equilateral, the third side also has a length of $2n$.

Thus, $2n + 2n + 2n = 96$, which can be simplified into $6n = 96$. After both sides are divided by 6, it can be determined that $n = 16$.

Module II

1. C: Use the formula for percentages:

$$percent = \frac{part}{whole}$$

$$= \frac{42}{48}$$

$$= 0.875 = 87.5\%$$

2. C: Use the formula for percent change:

$$percent\ change = \frac{amount\ of\ change}{original\ amount}$$

$$= \frac{7{,}375 - 7{,}250}{7{,}250} = 0.017 = 1.7\%$$

3. D: Plug in each set of values and determine if the inequality is true:

$$2(0) + 0 \leq -10\ FALSE$$

$$2(10) + 2 \leq -10\ FALSE$$

$$2(10) + 10 \leq -10\ FALSE$$

$$2(-10) + (-10) \leq -10\ TRUE$$

4. D: Factor the equation and set each factor equal to 0:

$$y = 16 \times 3 - 48 \times 2$$

$$16 \times 2(x - 3) = 0$$

$$x = 0\ and\ x = 3$$

5. C: Set up a system of equations where d equals the number of dimes and q equals number of quarters.

$$d + q = 34$$

$$0.1d + 0.25q = 6.25$$

$$0.1d + 0.25(34 - d) = 6.25$$

$$d = 15$$

$$q = 34 - 15 = 19$$

6. C: One way to find the answer is to draw a picture:

Put 24 cans into groups of 4. One out of every 4 cans is diet (light gray), so there is 1 light gray can for every 3 dark gray cans. That leaves 18 dark gray cans (regular soda).

Alternatively, solve the problem using ratios:

$$\frac{regular}{total} = \frac{3}{4} = \frac{x}{24}$$

$$4x = 72$$

$$x = 18$$

7. D: Identify the important parts of the circle:

$$r = 3$$

length of minor arc $ACB = 5$

Plug these values into the formula for the length of an arc and solve for θ.

$$s = \frac{\theta}{360°} \times 2\pi r$$

$$5 = \frac{\theta}{360} \times 2\pi(3)$$

$$\frac{5}{6\pi} = \theta/360$$

$$\theta = 95.5°$$

$$m\angle AOB = 95.5°$$

8. C: Use the formula for percent change:

$$percent\ change = \frac{amount\ of\ change}{original\ amount}$$

$$= \frac{680 - 425}{425}$$

$$= \frac{255}{425} = 0.60 = 60\%$$

9. B: There are 16 ounces in a pound, so the baby's starting weight is 120 ounces. He gained 6 ounces per month, or 6t. So, the baby's weight will be his initial weight plus the amount gained for each month:

$$y = 6t + 120$$

10. D: Assign variables and write the ratios as fractions. Then, cross multiply to solve for the number of apples and oranges sold:

$$x = apples$$

$$\frac{apples}{bananas} = \frac{3}{2} = \frac{x}{20}$$

$$60 = 2$$

$$x = 30 \; apples$$

$$y = oranges$$

$$\frac{oranges}{bananas} = \frac{1}{2} = \frac{y}{20}$$

$$2y = 20$$

$$y = 10 \; oranges$$

To find the total, add the number of apples, oranges, and bananas together:

$$30 + 20 + 10 = 60 \; pieces \; of \; fruit$$

11. B: Calculate the discriminant:

$$B2 - 4AC = 22 - 4(1)(4) = -12$$

The discriminant is negative and A ≠ C, so it is an ellipse.

12. B: Add the base amount and the tax on the extra percentage of the person's income:

$$10,620 + 0.2(80,000 - 75,000) = \$11,620$$

13. D: The surface area will be the area of the square base plus the area of the four triangles:

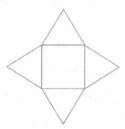

First, find the area of the square ($A = s2 \to 62 = 36$).

Then, to find the area of the triangles, first find the pyramid's slant height:

$$c2 = a2 + b2$$

$$l2 = 100 + 9$$

$$l = \sqrt{109}$$

Find the area of the triangle face using the slant height as the height of the triangle face:

$$A = \frac{1}{2} bh$$

$$A = \frac{1}{2} (6)(\sqrt{109})$$

$$A = 3\sqrt{109}$$

Finally, add the area of the square base and the four triangles to find the total surface area:

$$SA = 36 + 4(3\sqrt{109})$$

$$SA \approx 161.3 \; cm^2$$

14. D: Set up an equation: the original price (p) minus 30% of the original price is $385.

$$p - 0.3p = 385$$

$$p = \frac{385}{0.7} = \$550$$

15. A: Find the area of the room in square feet and convert it to square yards (1 square yard = 9 square feet). Then multiply by the cost per square yard.

$$area = 10 \times 12 = 120 \; square \; feet$$

$$\frac{120}{9} = \frac{40}{3} \; square \; yards$$

$$\frac{40}{3} \times \$12.51 = \frac{\$500.40}{3} = \$166.80$$

16. A: The amount of money in Jane's bank account can be represented by the expression 275 + 15h ($275 plus $15 for every hour she works). Therefore, the equation 400 = 275 + 15h describes how many hours she needs to babysit to have $400.

17. $5,000

Find Company X's profits for 2012 and 2013 from the bar graph:

$$2012 \; profit \approx \$15,000$$

$$2013 \; profit \approx \$20,000$$

Subtract to find the change in profit:

$$\$20,000 - \$15,000 = \$5,000$$

18. 1,954 points

Multiply the average number of points per game by the number of games he played:

$$26.4 \times 74 = 1953.6 \approx 1,954 \; points$$

19. 80

Write a formula to find the answer:

$$p = number\ of\ pages\ written\ by\ Chris$$

$$2p = number\ of\ pages\ written\ by\ Kim$$

$$p + 2p = 240$$

$$p = 80$$

Chris wrote 80 pages.

20. ≈ 13.59

The area of the shaded portion will be the area of the circle minus the area of the hexagon. Use the radius to find the area of the circle:

$$AC = \pi r^2$$

$$= \pi(5)^2$$

$$= 25\pi$$

To find the area of the hexagon, draw a right triangle from the vertex, and use special right triangles to find the hexagon's apothem. Then, use the apothem to calculate the area.

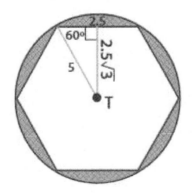

$$a = 2.5\sqrt{3}$$

$$A_H = \frac{ap}{2}$$

$$= \frac{(2.5\sqrt{3})(30)}{2}$$

$$= 64.95$$

Subtract the area of the hexagon from the circle to find the area of the shaded region.

$$= AC - AH$$

$$= 25\pi - 2.5\sqrt{3}$$

$$\approx 13.59$$

21. 4:00 p.m.

At 4:00 p.m., the temperature started to change the most, dropping rapidly from 4 to 5 p.m. This can be determined by subtracting the temperature values from 4:00 p.m. and 5:00 p.m., or by observing that the line connecting the values at 4 and 5 is the steepest on the graph.

22. $1,500

Set up a system of equations and solve using elimination:

$$f = \text{the cost of a financial stock}$$

$$a = \text{the cost of an auto stock}$$

$$50f + 10a = 1,300$$

$$10f + 10a = 500$$

$$50f + 10 = 1,300 \pm 50f - 50a = -2,500 = -40a = -1,200$$

$$a = 30$$

$$50(30) = 1,500$$

Practice Test #2
Reading and Writing

Module I

1. *"Many a man," says De Quincey, "can trace his ___ to a murder, of which, perhaps, he thought little enough at the time." This remark applies with peculiar force to Philip II of Spain, to his secretary, Antonio Perez, to the steward of Perez, to his page, and to a number of professional ruffians. All of these, from the King to his own scullion, were concerned in the slaying of Juan de Escovedo, secretary of Philip's famous natural brother, Don John of Austria. All of them, in different degrees, had bitter reason to regret a deed which, at the moment, seemed a commonplace political incident.*

Which option completes the text with the MOST logical and precise word or phrase?
- A) source of power
- B) salvation
- C) ruin
- D) creation

2. *When I was well grown, at last, I was sold and taken away, and I never saw her again. She was broken-hearted, and so was I, and we cried; but she comforted me as well as she could, and said we were sent into this world for a wise and good purpose, and must do our duties without repining, take our life as we might find it, live it for the best good of others, and never mind about the results; they were not our affair.*

As used in the text, what does the word *repining* MOST nearly mean?
- A) fretting
- B) finding a purpose
- C) forgetting
- D) losing

3. *Lo! in the orient when the gracious light*

   Lifts up his burning head, each under eye

   Doth homage to his new-appearing sight,

   Serving with looks his sacred majesty;

   And having climb'd the steep-up heavenly hill,

   Resembling strong youth in his middle age,

   Yet mortal looks adore his beauty still,

Attending on his golden pilgrimage:

But when from highmost pitch, with weary car,

Like feeble age, he reeleth from the day,

The eyes, 'fore duteous, now converted are

From his low tract, and look another way:

So thou, thyself outgoing in thy noon:

Unlook'd, on diest unless thou get a son.

Which option BEST states the main purpose of the text?
- A) to present a sunny view of a pilgrimage through the East
- B) to urge its subject to have a child so he will not be forgotten in death
- C) to describe the progression from golden youth to old age
- D) to compare a human life to the phases of the day

4. *Though riverside folk have never doubted that the elvers are young eels which have been hatched from spawn deposited by parent eels in the sea, and are "running up" to feed and grow to maturity in the rivers and streams inland, yet country folk away from the big rivers have queer notions as to the origin and breeding of eels. They catch large, plump eels a couple of feet long in stagnant ponds hundreds of miles from the sea, far from rivers, and more than a thousand feet above the sea-level.*

Which option BEST states the function of the underlined sentence in the text as a whole?
- A) It provides context for an earlier statement.
- B) It clarifies a muddy point from the first sentence.
- C) It suggests an alternate explanation to an earlier supposition.
- D) It provides specifics about an earlier implication in the text.

5. Text 1

Cats have been loved by noted persons through the centuries. Mahomet cut off the sleeve of his robe rather than awaken the pet cat who slept upon it. Petrarch loved his cat and had it embalmed at death. Montaigne could do his best writing only when his left hand fondled his cat.

Text 2

If you agree that we cannot treat men like machines, why should we put animals in that class? Why should we fall into the colossal ignorance and conceit of cataloging every human-like action of animals under the word instinct? *Man delights in thinking of himself as only a little lower than the angels. Then why should he not consider the animals as only a little lower than himself?*

Based on the texts, how would the author of Text 2 MOST likely describe the treatment of cats described in Text 1?
- A) The author of Text 2 would say that this treatment of cats was a bit over the top because people do not often treat each other with such care.
- B) The author of Text 2 would most likely say that the cats in question were worthy of this respect.
- C) The author of Text 2 would find it silly to act so devoted to mere cats.
- D) The author of Text 2 would not care how these pet cats were treated.

Module I

6. *The theory of relativity has justly excited a great amount of public attention. But, for all its importance, it has not been the topic which has chiefly _____ the recent interest of physicists.*

Which option completes the text with the MOST logical and precise word or phrase?
   A) eschewed
   B) disturbed
   C) absorbed
   D) avoided

7. *She mounted a box and watched the battle, her hands clenched, her eyes blazing, her heart sick; for her Cecil was getting the worst of it. He looked as sturdy as a little oak, and he planted his blows scientifically; but his antagonist was twice his size, lean and wiry, and full of nervous fire. Moreover, the surrounding influences were all for the American: Cecil was not only English, but he had snubbed these boys of Mrs. Hayne's boarding-house for three consecutive weeks. Vengeance had been in the air for some time.*

Which option BEST describes the overall structure of the text?
   A) It presents the narrative of a schoolyard fight.
   B) It begins with a description of fighting and progresses to a reflection on the concept.
   C) It begins with a description of Cecil and ends with an explanation of the reason for the fight he is currently in.
   D) It details the thoughts that the protagonist is having about Cecil and the fight he is in.

8. *That is to say, as I understand, that moods and tastes and fashions change; people fancy now this and now that; but what is unpretentious and what is true is always beautiful and good, and nothing else is so. This is not saying that fantastic and monstrous and artificial things do not please; everybody knows that they do please immensely for a time, and then, after the lapse of a much longer time, they have the charm of the rococo.*

Which option BEST states the main idea of the text?
   A) Rococo art shares a certain charm with the beauty of what is unpretentious.
   B) That which is straightforward and honest will always be good, unaffected by changes in fashion.
   C) The moods and tastes of people shift over time, but that which no longer pleases will eventually regain its charm.
   D) The only thing that remains certain in fashion is that tastes will change.

9. *Whether to follow the order of time or the order of subjects was a question which presented itself; and, as neither alternative promised satisfactory results, I eventually decided to compromise—to follow partly the one order and partly the other. The first volume is made up of essays in which the idea of evolution, general or special, is dominant. In the second volume, essays dealing with philosophical questions, with abstract and concrete science, and with aesthetics, are brought together; but though all of them are tacitly evolutionary, _____.*

Which option MOST logically completes the text?
   A) their evolutionism is an incidental rather than a necessary trait
   B) their evolutionism is their only essential trait
   C) none of them are as evolutionary as they seem
   D) none of them include discussion of aesthetics

10. Wuthering Heights *is an 1847 novel by Emily Brontë. Brontë portrays the character of Mr. Lockwood as silly and unable or unwilling to take a hint in interactions like this one with his new landlord, Heathcliff, who is clearly uninterested in becoming his friend: _____.*

Which quotation from *Wuthering Heights* MOST effectively illustrates the claim?

A) *"Mr. Lockwood, your new tenant, sir. I do myself the honor of calling as soon as possible after my arrival, to express the hope that I have not inconvenienced you by my perseverance in soliciting the occupation of Thrushcross Grange: I heard yesterday you had had some thoughts—"*

B) *When he saw my horse's breast fairly pushing the barrier, he did put out his hand to unchain it, and then sullenly preceded me up the causeway, calling, as we entered the court,—"Joseph, take Mr. Lockwood's horse; and bring up some wine."*

C) *In all England, I do not believe that I could have fixed on a situation so completely removed from the stir of society. A perfect misanthropist's Heaven—and Mr. Heathcliff and I are such a suitable pair to divide the desolation between us. A capital fellow!*

D) *The "walk in" was uttered with closed teeth, and expressed the sentiment, "Go to the Deuce!" Even the gate over which he leant manifested no sympathizing movement to the words; and I think that circumstance determined me to accept the invitation: I felt interested in a man who seemed more exaggeratedly reserved than myself.*

11. Homes Sold in Coral City 2010 – 2019

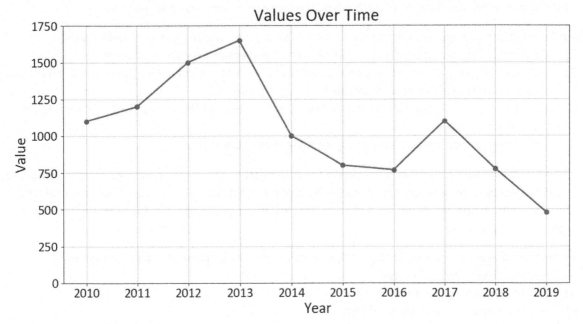

This graph shows the number of homes sold per year in Coral City, Utah, from 2010 – 2019. The x-axis shows the years during this range, and the y-axis counts the number of homes sold. According to an analyst, although the number of houses purchased each year has varied significantly over the period shown, <u>the number overall has fallen since 2010</u>.

Which option MOST effectively uses data from the graph to justify the underlined claim?
   A) The greatest annual number of homes sold during the period shown is about 1,000 in 2017.
   B) The smallest annual number of homes sold during the period shown is about 1,600 in 2013.
   C) About 1,000 homes were sold in 2010 and about 500 in 2019.
   D) About 1,000 homes were sold in 2010 and about 1,600 in 2013.

12. *Does the public for such a theatre exist? I think so. The number of playgoers is very large, and although _____, a very large proportion has grown weary of the ordinary drama—a fact shown by the recent failure of plays which not many years ago would have been successful.*

Which option MOST logically completes the text?
   A) only a comparatively small proportion goes out of its way to patronize the noncommercial drama
   B) a large portion goes out of its way to patronize the noncommercial drama
   C) none of these playgoers go out of their way to patronize the noncommercial drama
   D) there are more playgoers than cricket players

13. *An independent research group is conducting an experiment on adults with an underdeveloped pons, a part of the brain developed during the first six months of life. These adults have a heightened fight/flight reflex due to dysfunction in the pons. The researchers have hypothesized that these adults can lessen the developmental gap by engaging in "tummy time" the way that an infant would. The researchers have assigned daily "tummy time" to an experimental group of people with an*

underdeveloped pons and requested that a control group go about their daily routine as normal, and they intend to test the functioning of each participant's pons at the end of six months.

Which finding from the experiment, if true, would BEST support the researchers' hypothesis?
- A) The experimental and control group's final test results both show improvement.
- B) The control group maintained similar initial and final test results, while the "tummy time" group showed a decreased sensitivity of the fight/flight reflex.
- C) The "tummy time" group showed an increased sensitivity of the flight/flight reflex while the control group did not.
- D) The control group was the only group that showed improvement.

14. *The raw afternoon is rawest, and the dense fog is densest, _____ near that leaden-headed old obstruction, appropriate ornament for the threshold of a leaden-headed old corporation, Temple Bar. And hard by Temple Bar, in Lincoln's Inn Hall, at the very heart of the fog, sits the Lord High Chancellor in his High Court of Chancery.*

Which option completes the text so that it conforms to the conventions of Standard English?
- A) and the streets are full of mud
- B) and the mud clings to boots in the street
- C) and the muddy streets are muddiest
- D) the streets still muddier

15. *Examination of the photosphere shows that the outer surface is never at rest. Small bright cloudlets come and go in rapid succession, giving _____.*

Which option completes the text so that it conforms to the conventions of Standard English?
- A) the surface, through contrasts in luminosity, a granular appearance
- B) the surface, through contrasts in luminosity a granular appearance
- C) the surface through contrasts in luminosity, a granular appearance
- D) the surface; through contrasts in luminosity, a granular appearance

16. *Benjamin had three children: a son who died, some years after his father's disappearance, in consequence of a fall from a horse at a race _____, who was drowned in the Tiber; and another who married the Earl of Castlestuart in 1830, and after his death married Signor Pistocchi.*

Which option completes the text so that it conforms to the conventions of Standard English?
- A) in Rome a daughter
- B) in Rome – a daughter
- C) in Rome, a daughter
- D) in Rome; a daughter

17. *Heat plays an important part in the splitting of rocks and in the formation of debris. Rocks in exposed places ___ greatly affected by changes in temperature, and in regions where the changes in temperature are sudden, severe, and frequent, the rocks are not able to withstand the strain of expansion and contraction, and as a result crack and split.*

Which option completes the text so that it conforms to the conventions of Standard English?

- A) were
- B) are
- C) have been
- D) used to be

18. *She gave me plenty of food, put good clothes upon me, and told me to go and play with her own ___ remained but a short time at Sau-ge-nong.*

Which option completes the text so that it conforms to the conventions of Standard English?

- A) sons. We
- B) sons? We
- C) sons: We
- D) sons, we

19. *It was a matter of chance that I should have rented a house in one of the strangest communities in North America. It was on that slender riotous island which extends itself due east of _____ other natural curiosities, two unusual formations of land.*

Which option completes the text so that it conforms to the conventions of Standard English?

- A) New York and where there are among
- B) New York—and where there are—among
- C) New York, and where there are—among
- D) New York—and where there are, among

20. *"It was already sufficiently difficult," says Arago, "to imagine what could be the kind of change in the constitution of the globe which could act during one hundred and fifty-three years in gradually transferring the direction of the magnetic needle from due north to 23° west of north. We see that it is now necessary to explain, _____, how it has happened that this gradual change has ceased and has given place to a return towards the preceding state of the globe."*

Which option completes the text with the MOST logical transition?

- A) despite this
- B) nevertheless
- C) however
- D) moreover

21. *Gentlemanliness, however, in ordinary parlance, must be taken to signify those qualities which are usually the evidence of high breeding, and which, so far as they can be acquired, it should be every man's effort to acquire; or, if he has them by nature, to preserve and exalt. Vulgarity, _____, will signify qualities usually characteristic of ill-breeding, which, according to his power, becomes every person's duty to subdue.*

Which option completes the text with the MOST logical transition?
- A) similarly
- B) on the other hand
- C) afterward
- D) nevertheless

22. While researching a topic, a student has taken the following notes:
- *The brontosaurus was an herbivorous sauropod dinosaur of the Late Jurassic period, and its habitat was in present-day United States.*

- *Brontosaurus was large, long-necked, and quadrupedal and had a long, whip-like tail.*

- *Brontosaurus means "thunder lizard," a combination of the Greek words brontē (thunder) and sauros (lizard).*

- *American paleontologist Othniel Charles Marsh first described it in 1879 based on a partial skeleton found in Como Bluff, Wyoming.*

- *The three known species of brontosaurus are: the first, B. excelsus; B. parvus, discovered in 1902; and B. yahnahpin, discovered in 1994.*

The student wants to explain the origin of the dinosaur's name. Which option MOST effectively uses relevant information from the notes to accomplish this goal?
- A) Brontosaurus, the great "thunder lizard," was a large, long-necked, quadrupedal beast with a long, whip-like tail.
- B) Perhaps owing to its impressive size, the species was given a name that means "thunder lizard," a combination of the Greek words *brontē* (thunder) and *sauros* (lizard).
- C) The brontosaurus was first described in 1879 based on a partial skeleton found in Como Bluff, Wyoming.
- D) Brontosaurus excelsus was the first species of brontosaurus discovered in 1879.

23. *He alone will know that the principle he has to elucidate and apply is living, organic. It is indeed the very principle of artistic creation itself. _____ he will approach what claims to be a work of art first as a thing in itself, and seek with it the most intimate and immediate contact in order that he may decide whether it too is organic and living.*

Which option completes the text with the MOST logical transition?
- A) Therefore,
- B) Nevertheless,
- C) Even so,
- D) Despite this,

24. While researching a topic, a student has taken the following notes:
- *In Cold Blood: A True Account of a Multiple Murder and Its Consequences is a 1966 book by Truman Capote.*
- *The work was inspired by a 300-word article that ran in the New York Times in November 1959 about the unexplained murder of the Clutter family in rural Holcomb, Kansas.*
- *Capote spent the next few years becoming acquainted with anyone involved in the investigation as well as most of the residents of the area.*
- *Capote claimed to have tested at "over 90 percent" accuracy in recalling verbatim conversations, and instead of taking notes during interviews, he relied on his memory to write down quotes afterward.*
- *Various Kansas residents who spoke to Capote have claimed that he mischaracterized or misquoted them in his book.*

The student wants to draw attention to the flaws in Capote's approach to this project. Which option MOST effectively uses relevant information from the notes to accomplish this goal?
- A) While various Kansas residents who spoke to Capote claimed that he mischaracterizes or misquotes them in his book, the work directly resulted in the capture and execution of the killers.
- B) The original 300-word article that ran in the *New York Times* in November 1959 about the unexplained murder of the Clutter family in rural Holcomb, Kansas, did not receive the kind of sensational attention that Capote's book did.
- C) If Capote was truly "over 90 percent" accurate in his recall of verbatim conversations, perhaps the remaining percentage accounts for residents' claims that the quotes he wrote down by memory were inaccurate.
- D) Capote tested at "over 90 percent" accuracy in recalling verbatim conversations and spent several years becoming acquainted with anyone involved in the investigation as well as most residents of the area.

25. *It will also have been made clear that hundreds of such engravings, more or less fragmentary, are known. Some are very skillful works of art, others of a much inferior quality. Many, _____, show an astonishing familiarity with the animal drawn and a sureness of drawing which is not surpassed by the work of modern artists (see Chapter III).*

Which option completes the text with the MOST logical transition?
- A) in consequence
- B) as a result
- C) to a point
- D) however

26. While researching a topic, a student has taken the following notes:
- *Maria Callas was an American-born soprano who received her musical education in Greece starting at 13 years old.*
- *She sang repertoire ranging from classical opera seria to bel canto operas like those of Donizetti, Bellini, and Rossini.*
- *She was known as La Divina ("The Divine One") for her musical and dramatic talents.*

- *She lost a large amount of weight in the middle of her career, which some believe contributed to her vocal decline, ending her career prematurely.*

- *The press enjoyed reporting on her temperamental behavior and the love affair between her and Greek shipping tycoon Aristotle Onassis.*

The student wants to introduce Callas to an audience unfamiliar with the artist. Which option MOST effectively uses relevant information from the notes to accomplish this goal?

    A) Donizetti, Bellini, and Rossini are only three examples of the composers whose work Maria Callas sang during her career.

    B) Maria Callas began her musical education at 13 years old and went on to be known as *La Divina* ("The Divine One") before the vocal decline that ended her career prematurely.

    C) Callas was known as *La Divina* ("The Divine One") for her musical and dramatic talents, which she displayed in such wide-ranging repertoire as classical opera seria and the bel canto operas of Donizetti, Bellini, and Rossini.

    D) Callas has become known as the original diva for her temperamental behavior, which overshadowed her considerable talent.

27. While researching a topic, a student has taken the following notes:

- *The Stanford Prison Experiment was a psychological experiment conducted in August 1971.*

- *The experiment entailed a two-week simulation of a prison environment that examined the effects of situational variables on participants' behavior.*

- *Volunteers selected as "guards" were given uniforms to de-individuate them and were told to prevent prisoners from escaping, while the "prisoners" were arrested by real Palo Alto police.*

- *The experiment was shut down on its sixth day due to increasingly brutal psychological abuse of the prisoners by the guards during the first five days.*

- *Psychologist Peter Gray argued in 2012 that the study encouraged participants to do what they believed the researchers wanted them to do, acting out the stereotypical roles of prisoners and guards.*

The student wants to present this experiment as an example of an unethical psychological experiment. Which option MOST effectively uses relevant information from the notes to accomplish this goal?

    A) Psychologist Peter Gray argued in 2012 that the increasingly brutal psychological abuse of the prisoners by the guards during those first five days was due to the study encouraging participants to do what they believed the researchers wanted them to do: acting out the stereotypical roles of prisoners and guards.

    B) The Stanford Prison Experiment, conducted in August 1971, involved participants acting as "prisoners" who were arrested by real Palo Alto police to begin their fake imprisonment.

    C) The experiment was completely unethical, involving a two-week simulation of a prison environment that examined the effects of situational variables on participants' behavior.

    D) The experiment took place in August, one of the hottest months of the year, which likely did not improve participants' moods.

Module II

1. *I am very conscious of the manifold _____ of these volumes. They are the work, not of a professed student, but of one who only plays at scholarship in the rare intervals of a busy administrative life.*

Which option completes the text with the MOST logical and precise word or phrase?
   A) iterations
   B) accomplishments
   C) imperfections
   D) protrusions

2. *Many anecdotes are current in Lamar County, illustrating the primitive methods of pedagogy as pursued by Allen Burrow. It is said that the elder Graves, who had several sons as pupils, withdrew the hopeful scions of the Graves household from the school for the reason that after six months' tuition, he having incidentally enrolled the whole contingent in a spelling bee, they all insisted on spelling every monosyllable ending with a consonant by adding an extra one, as d-o-g-g, dog; b-u-g-g, bug.*

As used in the text, what does the word *pedagogy* MOST nearly mean?
   A) teaching
   B) writing
   C) science
   D) logic

3. *However this may be, the main point is that sufficient knowledge has now been acquired of vital phenomena, to justify the assertion that the notion that there is anything exceptional about these phenomena, receives not a particle of support from any known fact. On the contrary, there is a vast and an increasing mass of evidence that birth and death, health and disease, are as much parts of the ordinary stream of events as the rising and setting of the sun, or the changes of the moon; and that the living body is a mechanism, the proper working of which we term health; its disturbance, disease; its stoppage, death.*

Which option BEST states the main purpose of the text?
   A) to demand respect for the idea that there are concepts that science cannot explain
   B) to question the assertion that there is no supernatural explanation for the processes of human life
   C) to explain the reason that human health should be studied in the same way as the changes of the moon
   D) to argue that there is no support for a supernatural explanation of the processes of human life

4. *The facts of the matter are simply these: <u>Some years ago I became seriously ill, grew worse day by day, and was pronounced dying, and finally dead.</u> Dead I apparently was, and dead I remained to all intents and purposes for the greater part of two days, after which, to the intense and utter astonishment of my friends and of the physicians, I exhibited symptoms of returning vitality, and in the course of a week or two was convalescent.*

Which option BEST states the function of the underlined sentence in the text as a whole?
- A) It elaborates on the statement made in the previous sentence.
- B) It presents information promised in the previous sentence.
- C) It changes the topic from the one in the previous sentence to that of the following sentence.
- D) It prevents the following sentence from seeming too far-fetched.

5. Text 1

Mysticism is the outbreak in man of a spiritual element which cannot be ignored, cannot be wholly suppressed, and is man's noblest element when rightly directed and balanced. It is capable of regulation, but unregulated, it may become even a mischievous faculty.

Text 2

Mysticism does not maintain that such things as cruelty, for example, are good, but it denies that they are real: they belong to that lower world of phantoms from which we are to be liberated by the insight of the vision.

Based on the texts, which option BEST describes what the author of Text 1 might say about the specific aspect of mysticism presented in Text 2?
- A) Mysticism is not a concept separate from the ideas of good and evil but rather a system of rules and precepts.
- B) Stating that mysticism as a concept holds itself separate from the ideas of good and evil is an example of the lack of regulation that could lead to mischief.
- C) The idea that mysticism as a concept is detached from the concepts of good and evil is inaccurate because mysticism is capable of regulation.
- D) This ideological detachment of mysticism from the concepts of good and evil could feed into a lack of regulation that would lead to its practices being put to ill use.

6. *When he started from England for Switzerland in February 1669, Marsilly left in London a valet, called by him "Martin," who had quitted his service and was living with his own family. This man is the "Eustache Dauger" of our mystery. The name is his prison _____, as "Lestang" was that of Mattioli.*

Which option completes the text with the MOST logical and precise word or phrase?
- A) racket
- B) vocation
- C) pseudonym
- D) friend

7. *Fog of the color known as pea-soup—in reality amber mixed with lemon-peel and delicately tinted with smut—pervaded the genial shades of Kensington Gardens and cast a halo of breathless romance over many a "long, unlovely street" and many a towering pile of crudely hideous flats in the regions round about. It sneaked down chimneys, stalked insolently through front doors, regardless of locks, curtains, and screens; it wandered noiselessly about houses, penetrating even to my lady's chamber; it permeated cosy drawing-rooms and snug dining-rooms with gloom like that of an ancestral ghost, or an unforgettable sorrow, or—the haunting horror of unpaid bills.*

Which option BEST describes the overall structure of the text?
- A) It uses the movement of fog to propel a dynamic description of the places and objects the fog touches.
- B) It sketches an image of fog in the night, followed by an image of the interior of a lady's house.
- C) It presents alternating descriptions of Kensington Gardens and the run-down houses in a less savory part of town.
- D) It tells the story of a sentient fog character making its way in the world.

8.

Participants' Responses about AI Performance When Used for Different Purposes			
Purpose	Mildly or Very Bad (%)	Neutral (%)	Mildly or Very Good (%)
Screenwriting	89	2	9
Visual art creation	76	3	21
Navigation	13	3	84

The Channel Ten News team sent correspondents to poll members of the public to find out how effective they felt AI was or would be at performing various tasks. The table shows the participants' opinions of how well AI would perform when used for three purposes. The strongest point of similarity between the participants' responses _____.

Which option MOST effectively uses data from the table to complete the example?
- A) when asked about navigation and screenwriting was how many people thought AI made a mess of things
- B) regardless of the purpose they were being asked about was that neutral opinions of AI performance were exceedingly rare
- C) when asked about screenwriting and visual art creation was how overwhelmingly negative the responses were, with 86 percent feeling that AI should not be involved with visual art creation
- D) was how favorably they viewed AI overall

9. *World Book Company, whose motto is "The Application of the World's Knowledge to the World's Needs," has been much in sympathy with the movement to make science an integral part of our elementary education, so that all our people from the highest to the lowest will be able to use it for themselves and to appreciate the possibilities of ameliorating the conditions of human life by its application to the problems that confront us. We count it our good fortune, therefore, that we are able at this time to offer Common Science to the schools. It is one of the new types of texts that are built on educational research and not by guess, _____.*

Which option MOST logically completes the text?
   A)   and that is the reason for its higher cost, which many schools may find prohibitive
   B)   and it is the only textbook currently available that is able to make this claim
   C)   and we believe it to be a substantial contribution to the teaching of the subject
   D)   which increases the likelihood of its obsolescence in the coming years

10. *It is probably known to most readers that there is a distinction between tradition and saga. Tradition has, or at least seems to have, to do with facts, usually designating some particular spot or region where the incident is said to have taken place, often even giving the names of actors, while the saga is entirely free in its scope, equally as regards incident, and the time and place of its happening. Not infrequently the traditions of a people are founded upon actual historical occurrences, which, often repeated in the naïve manner of the peasantry, become, finally, folk-lore. A great many are, however, drawn from ancient myths, which, in time, become clad in historical garb, and are located in some particular place.*

Which option BEST states the main idea of the text?
   A)   Tradition differs from saga in citing a particular location as its setting and giving the names of the people involved in the story.
   B)   Saga is free in its scope and does not designate any particular spot or region where the incident is said to have taken place.
   C)   Ancient myths have often been transformed into tradition over time.
   D)   Tradition is less dependent in its telling upon a particular time or place than is saga.

11. *When did the first potter live? The world (as Sir Henry Taylor has oracularly told us) knows nothing of its greatest men; and the very name of the father of all potters has been utterly forgotten in the lapse of ages. Indeed, paradoxical as it may sound to say so, one may reasonably doubt whether there was ever actually any one single man on whom one could definitely lay one's finger, and say with confidence, "Here we have the first potter."*

Which option BEST states the main idea of the text?
   A)   Potters are by and large not given enough credit for their work.
   B)   Potters generally live anonymous lives and are forgotten by history.
   C)   The name of the first potter should be found and celebrated.
   D)   Nobody knows for sure the identity of the first potter.

12. *A group of psychology graduate students are conducting an experiment to determine the impact of the expressiveness of hiring managers' faces during job interviews on the stress levels of applicants. The student research team recruited several participants to experience a mock job interview, either with a team member who would engage in lively conversation or a member who would remain deliberately stone-faced and give one-word responses to questions whenever possible. They then asked participants about their stress levels before and after the interview. The team hypothesized that the participants would be significantly more stressed in the second scenario.*

Which quotation from a participant who interacted with a stone-faced interviewer would BEST support the graduate students' hypothesis?
- A) "I am just always stressed about job interviews, no matter what."
- B) "I liked that the interviewer wasn't trying so hard to be nice for once. He looked like he wanted to be there as little as I imagine they always do."
- C) "It was unnerving the way the interviewer just stared at me and didn't laugh at any of my jokes. I'm normally not this stressed after a job interview, but I'm still sweating."
- D) "It was annoying how the interviewer didn't add anything to the conversation."

13. *Although I am quite ready to admit that these points involve great and unsolved difficulties, I am unable to agree with Nicholson's conclusions. In the first place, his calculations rest upon a particular application to non-circular orbits of the principle of constancy of angular momentum for each electron, which it does not seem possible to justify either on the quantum theory or on the ordinary mechanics, _____.*

Which option MOST logically completes the text?
- A) but is the only logical conclusion given the evidence Nicholson has cited
- B) and which has no direct connection with the assumptions used in my papers
- C) so Nicholson's conclusions make sense on that count
- D) which does not pose an issue when it comes to my agreement with the aforementioned conclusions

14. *And now, dear Margaret, do I not deserve to accomplish some great _____ might have been passed in ease and luxury, but I preferred glory to every enticement that wealth placed in my path.*

Which option completes the text so that it conforms to the conventions of Standard English?
- A) purpose. My life
- B) purpose? My life
- C) purpose: My life
- D) purpose; my life

15. *In spite of a temperamental leaning to anarchism, I am persuaded that an industrial world cannot maintain itself against internal disruptive forces without a great deal more organization than we have at present. It is not the amount of organization, but _____, that cause our troubles.*

Which option completes the text so that it conforms to the conventions of Standard English?
- A) one's kind and one's purposes
- B) his kinds and his purposes
- C) their kind and their purposes
- D) its kind and its purposes

16. *We have seen that Strabo, who wrote and travelled during the reigns of the first two Roman emperors, _____ the earliest author who mentions the fall of the Colossus of Rhodes, and that very concisely. Pliny enters into somewhat fuller details and speaks of the dimensions of the mutilated limbs.*

Which option completes the text so that it conforms to the conventions of Standard English?
   A) was after Polybius
   B) was after Polybius,
   C) was, after Polybius,
   D) was, after Polybius

17. *If I have convinced anyone present that science has still a good deal up her sleeve, and that of a sufficiently startling character, I shall be amply repaid. If anything I have said appears to be of a gratuitously disgusting nature, I would reply that _____ of normal life do seem to many to be of that nature, and that these phenomena are of the utmost scientific and practical importance.*

Which option completes the text so that it conforms to the conventions of Standard English?
   A) certain phenomena
   B) certain phenomenon
   C) a certain phenomena
   D) certain phenomenas

18. *This was the time when he had been gathering materials for a History of the Council of Trent. That this cleavage, coming when it did, had a paralyzing ___ on Acton's productive energy is most probable, for it made him feel that he was no longer one of a school, and was without sympathy and support in the things that lay nearest his heart.*

Which option completes the text so that it conforms to the conventions of Standard English?
   A) affect
   B) affects
   C) effects
   D) effect

19. *The Locrians were laid waste by a legate of Scipio, yet they were not avenged by him, nor was the insolence of the legate punished, owing entirely to his easy nature. Insomuch that someone in the Senate, wishing to excuse him, said there were _____ than to correct the errors of others.*

Which option completes the text so that it conforms to the conventions of Standard English?
   A) many men who knew much better how not to err
   B) many men, who knew much better how not to err,
   C) many men, who knew much better how not to err
   D) many men; who knew much better how not to err

20. *Other objections, also, were incidentally alluded to by medieval writers. _____, it was said, the supreme question in all matters of life is the question of conduct, and it was not apparent in what manner poetry conduces to action. Poetry has no practical use; it rather enervates men than urges them to the call of duty; and above all, there are more profitable occupations in which the righteous man may be engaged.*

Which option completes the text with the MOST logical transition?
- A) However
- B) By contrast
- C) For comparison's sake
- D) For example

21. *Pure carbonic acid gas is the heaviest of all the gases. That which is sent out of the lungs is not pure, because the whole of the air taken into the lungs at the previous inspiration has not been deprived of its oxygen, and the nitrogen is returned. _____ the breath sent out of the lungs may be said to consist of air, with a large proportion of carbonic acid gas.*

Which option completes the text with the MOST logical transition?
- A) Therefore,
- B) Nevertheless,
- C) Previously,
- D) In addition,

22. While researching a topic, a student has taken the following notes:
- *The Iwo Jima rail, a subspecies of the white-browed crake, was a semi-amphibious bird native to the island of Iwo Jima.*
- *It was dark brown with a black mottled back and a white belly.*
- *The bird was generally about six inches long.*
- *Forest clearance for sugarcane farming is thought to have contributed to the extinction of the bird.*
- *The last specimen of it was collected in 1911, and its last reported sightings were in 1924.*

The student wants to describe the appearance of the Iwo Jima rail. Which option MOST effectively uses relevant information from the notes to accomplish this goal?
- A) The Iwo Jima rail was a subspecies of the white-browed crake.
- B) It typically measured about six inches in length and had a dark brown coloration with black mottles on its back and a white belly.
- C) Forest clearance for sugarcane farming is thought to have contributed to the extinction of the bird.
- D) The last specimen of the Iwo Jima rail was collected in 1911, and its last reported sightings were in 1924.

23. *He hurried back to the village and gave the alarm by firing a gun. _____, however, a young man belonging to a neighboring town, who had been spending the night with a young woman of the village, had met the advance of the war-party, and, turning back in extreme terror and confusion, thought only of the safety of his betrothed, and passed silently through a considerable part of the village to her dwelling.*

Which option completes the text with the MOST logical transition?
A) Previous to this
B) As a result of this
C) In response to this
D) Similarly

24. While researching a topic, a student has taken the following notes:
- *The Internal Family Systems Model (IFS) was created by Richard C. Schwartz in the 1980s to offer an integrative approach to individual psychotherapy.*

- *IFS uses systems psychology as developed for family therapy and operates on the theory that a person's true Self lies underneath a "family" of inner parts in the mind.*

- *IFS maintains that all parts have a positive intent, even if their actions cause dysfunction.*

- *The first type of "part" is the Exile, which carries pain and fear from childhood trauma and becomes isolated from the rest of the system.*

- *The second type is the Manager, which protects the mind by managing interactions with the world to prevent trauma from overwhelming a person's conscious awareness.*

- *The third type is the Firefighter, which diverts attention away from the Exiles when they break out and can lead to poor coping behaviors like overeating or drug use.*

The student wants to explain the three main types of "parts" in an IFS system to an audience who is already familiar with the general theory. Which option MOST effectively uses relevant information from the notes to accomplish this goal?
A) In IFS, there are three types of "parts": Exiles, Managers, and Firefighters.
B) In the Internal Family Systems (IFS) model, created by Richard C. Schwartz in the 1980s to offer an integrative approach to individual psychotherapy, there are three types of "parts": Exiles, Managers, and Firefighters.
C) The job of the Exiles is to carry pain and fear from childhood trauma, and they become isolated from the rest of the system.
D) An Exile is a "part" that carries pain and fear from childhood trauma and thus becomes isolated from the system as a whole. Managers protect the mind by managing interactions with the world to prevent trauma from overwhelming a person's conscious awareness. Firefighters divert attention away from the Exiles when they break out.

25. *Bedford feared that these gentlemen might seize Gerberoy and make it tenable, so he dispatched one of his captains, the earl of Arundel, to intercept them. Arundel was approaching Gerberoy without having discovered any signs of the enemy; and there was apparently nothing to apprehend from a ruinous old stronghold which could not contain half as many men as he had at his back. _____ like a prudent general he sent forward Sir Ralph Standish with a hundred men to reconnoiter.*

Which option completes the text with the MOST logical transition?
    A) Accordingly,
    B) Nevertheless,
    C) Therefore,
    D) Due to this,

26. While researching a topic, a student has taken the following notes:
  • *Salvador Dalí was a Spanish surrealist artist known chiefly for his bizarre imagery and eccentric behavior.*

  • *He was born in Figueres, Catalonia, Spain, and he received his fine arts education in Madrid.*

  • *He joined the Surrealist group in 1929 and was soon one of its greatest exponents.*

  • *His best-known work is* The Persistence of Memory, *with its famous surreal imagery of melting clocks.*

  • *He finished painting* The Persistence of Memory *in August 1931.*

  • *He lived in the United States from 1940 to 1948 and achieved commercial success while there.*

The student wants to focus on *The Persistence of Memory*. Which option MOST effectively uses relevant information from the notes to accomplish this goal?
    A) Salvador Dalí, a Spanish surrealist artist known chiefly for his bizarre imagery and eccentric behavior, finished painting *The Persistence of Memory* in August 1931.
    B) While his best-known work is *The Persistence of Memory* (1931), with its famous surreal imagery of melting clocks, it was not until his move to America in 1940 that Salvador Dalí achieved commercial success.
    C) Salvador Dalí completed his best-known work in 1931—*The Persistence of Memory*—famous for its surreal imagery of melting clocks.
    D) Salvador Dalí joined the Surrealist group in 1929 and was soon one of its greatest exponents, eventually drawing serious attention to the movement with his famous painting *The Persistence of Memory*, known for its famous surreal imagery of melting clocks.

27. While researching a topic, a student has taken the following notes:

- *Nelle Harper Lee was an American novelist who wrote the widely beloved novel* To Kill a Mockingbird.

- *Lee won the 1961 Pulitzer Prize for* To Kill a Mockingbird.

- *Lee also helped her close friend Truman Capote with his research for his book* In Cold Blood.

- *Finch, the last name of the protagonist's family in* To Kill a Mockingbird, *was Lee's mother's maiden name.*

- *Scout Finch, the protagonist of the novel, is the child of respected small-town attorney Atticus Finch, which mirrors Lee's upbringing as the daughter of respected politician and lawyer Amasa Coleman Lee.*

The student wants to highlight the autobiographical elements of *To Kill a Mockingbird*. Which option MOST effectively uses relevant information from the notes to accomplish this goal?

A) Amasa Coleman Lee was a respected politician and lawyer, and Lee's mother's maiden name was Finch.
B) Scout Finch was the protagonist of the novel, which won the Pulitzer Prize in 1961.
C) Atticus Finch, Scout's father, sported Lee's mother's maiden name as well as the profession and reputation of Lee's father.
D) Lee further contributed to the publication of great literature when she helped her close friend Truman Capote with his research for his book *In Cold Blood*.

Practice Test #2
Math

For questions 1 – 16, work the problem and choose the most correct answer. For questions 17 – 22, work the problem and enter the correct answer in the space provided. You may use a calculator, but remember: some questions may be more efficiently answered through reasoning rather than the use of a calculator.

Module I

1. What is 5% of 0.5×880?
   A) 44
   B) 88
   C) 22
   D   11

2. Which equation has the same solution as the given equation?
$$15x - 5 = 100$$

   A) $5x - 1 = 20$
   B) $3x - 1 = 20$
   C) $2x - 5 = 20$
   D) $2x + 5 = 20$

3. The solution to the given system of equations is (x, y). What is the value of x?
$$y = 2x$$
$$6x - 2y = 12$$

   A) 8
   B) 4
   C) 2
   D) 6

4. Eli sold $84 worth of merchandise. His store consists of some items worth $4 and other items worth $12. Which equation represents this situation, where x represents the number of $4 items and y represents the number of $12 items?
   A) $12x + 4y = 84$
   B) $4x + 12y = 84$
   C) $12x - 4y = 84$
   D) $4x - 12y = 84$

5. Which expression is equivalent to $2x^8 2y^{12} + 4x^4 8y^4$?
   A) $2^2(x^2y^3 + 2x4y)$
   B) $2^4(x^4 2y^3 + 2x^2 4y)$
   C) $2^2(x^3y^4 + 2x4y^2)$
   D) $2^4(x^2y^3 + 2x4y)$

6. Which equation represents the line graph below?

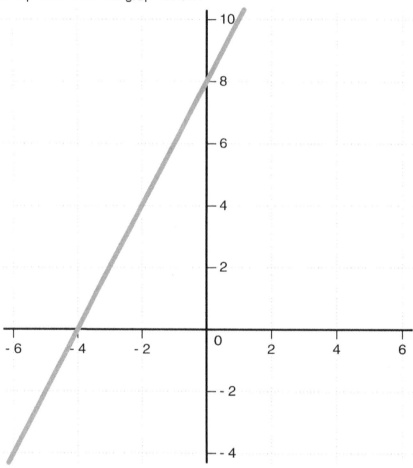

   A) $y = 2x + 4$
   B) $2y = 3x + 16$
   C) $3y + 4x = 8$
   D) $y = 2x + 8$

7. Which of the following equations is the MOST appropriate linear model for the data shown in the scatter plot?

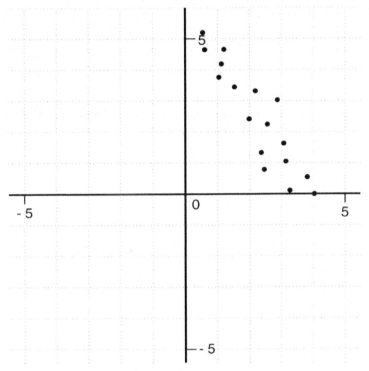

A) $y = -1.6x + 5.48$
B) $y = -1.6x - 5.48$
C) $y = 1.6x + 5.48$
D) $y = 1.6x - 5.48$

8. Circle A has a radius of $2n$ and Circle B has a radius of $124n$, in which n is a positive constant. The area of Circle B is how many times larger than the area of Circle A?
   A) 15,376
   B) 1,922
   C) 961
   D) 3,844

9. A large national park has an area of 234 square miles. What is the area, in square yards, of the national park? (1 mile = 1,760 yards)
   A) 411,840 miles
   B) 724,838,400 miles
   C) 362,419,200 miles
   D) 595,760,000 miles

10. The measure of angle P is $2\pi \div 4$ radians. The measure of angle J is $4\pi \div 16$ radians greater than the measure of angle P. What is the measure of angle J, in degrees?
    A) 46 degrees
    B) 89 degrees
    C) 135 degrees
    D) 156 degrees

11. In dollars, the total cost to adopt a puppy consists of a $500 adoption fee and $20 for each bag of food. Jonathan plans to adopt a puppy and spend a maximum of $700 on the adoption fee and food. Which inequality represents this situation?

    A) $20b + 700 \leq 500$
    B) $20b + 500 \leq 700$
    C) $500b + 20 \leq 700$
    D) $b + 520 \leq 700$

12. Right triangles JLH and PGK are similar, where J and L correspond to P and G, respectively. Angle L has a measure of 46°. What is the measure of angle P?

    A) 46°
    B) 44°
    C) 134°
    D) 89°

13. A grocery store has 12 aisles and 6 display cases. The total number of products in the store is 4,556. The equation $12x + 6y = 4,556$ represents this situation. Which of the following is the best interpretation of y in this context?

    A) the number of products per display case in the store
    B) the number of products per aisle in the store
    C) the average number of products in one aisle and one display case
    D) the total number of products in every display case

14. The frequency table below summarizes the 26 values in a data set. What is the MOST frequently occurring data value in the data set?

Data value	Frequency
4	9
5	6
7	2
9	1
5	4
113	8

    A) 4
    B) 5
    C) 9
    D) 113

---

15. A random drawing for a radio contest has 52 entrants, with 2 names for each letter of the alphabet. If the radio host pulls 2 names, what is the probability that both of those names start with the first 7 letters of the alphabet?

    A) $\frac{1}{7}$

    B) $\frac{2}{16}$

    C) $\frac{2}{7}$

    D) $\frac{7}{52}$

16. The function m is defined by $m(x) = 2x^2 - 7$. For which value of x is $m(x) = 121$?

    A) 12
    B) 7
    C) 6
    D) 8

17. A circle in the xy-plane has a diameter with endpoints $(3, 4)$ and $(2, 7)$. An equation of this circle is $(x - 4)^2 + (y - 6)^2 = r^2$, where r is a positive constant. What is the value of r?

18. Kevin is going to purchase a car. The sticker price of the car is $15,000. Gas, oil changes, and maintenance will cost Kevin $900 per year. Kevin wants to upgrade his car, but be cannot spend more than $18,250 this year. He writes an inequality to describe the situation as $15,000 + 900y + z \le 18,250$. What is the largest number that can define the value of z in Kevin's first year of car ownership?

19. The solution to the given system of equations is (x, y). What is the value of y?
$$x = 4y$$
$$6x - 2y = 66$$

20. A country is measuring its population growth. In 2010, there were 3,500,000 people. Due to a high birth rate, the country's population is projected to double at a constant rate by 2030 and continue at the same rate. How many million people will this country likely have in 2060?

21. Tom is purchasing a new wardrobe and is drawing a line graph to represent how much money he is able to spend on shirts and pants, depending on how many of each that he buys. Each shirt (x) costs $10 and each pair of pants (y) costs $20. He has a budget of $180. What is the slope of the line?

22. For line J, the table shows three values of x and their corresponding values of y. Line P is the result of translating line J up 6 units in the xy-plane. At which point on the x-axis would line P cross it?

x	y
16	122
22	146
30	178

Module II

1. Jane works an hourly job and earns d dollars for every hour that she works. Jane makes h dollars per hour. Which expression represents the amount of money that Jane makes after working 24 hours?
   A) $24 + h = d$
   B) $24h = d$
   C) $24d - h = 2d$
   D) $h - 24 = d$

2. The equation below represents the fuel efficiency of a modern sedan:

$$e = m \div g$$

If e represents total fuel efficiency, m represents the number of miles traveled, and g represents the gallons of gas consumed, how many gallons of gas does the sedan consume to travel 240 miles at a fuel efficiency of 30?
   A)   8
   B)   16
   C)   4
   D)   2

3. For the right triangle shown, $a = 3$ and $b = 2$. Which expression represents the value of c?

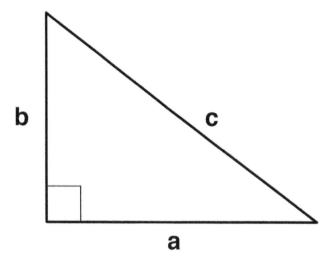

   A) $3 + 2$
   B) $\sqrt{3 + 2}$
   C) $\sqrt{3^2 + 2^2}$
   D) $3^3 + 2^2$

4. The function a is defined by $a(x) = 2x - 3$. What is the y-intercept of the graph of $y = a(x)$ in the xy-plane?
   A) $(-3, 0)$
   B) $(3, 0)$
   C) $(0, -3)$
   D) $(2, -3)$

5. Which expression is equivalent to $(4x^2 + 8x) - (-5x^2 + 2x)$?

A) $9x^2 + 6x$

B) $-x^2 + 6x$

C) $9x^2 + 10x$

D) $-20x^2 + 6x$

6. Which ordered pair (x, y) fits into the system of equations below?

$$x + 21 = 31$$

$$(2x + 4)^2 = 4y$$

A) $(2, 12)$

B) $(24, 288)$

C) $(10, 24)$

D) $(10, 144)$

7. A list of 13 data values is shown:

$$1, 3, 2, 5, 4, 6, 7, 2, 8, 8, 12, 5, 2$$

What is the mean of this data?

A) 2

B) 3

C) 4

D) 5

8. What is the MINIMUM value of the given function?

$$q(x) = x^3 + 23$$

A) 1

B) 23

C) 24

D) 552

9. Each year, Henry contributes to his retirement fund. The value of the fund increases by approximately 8% of its worth during that year. Which of the following functions BEST models how the value of the investment changes over time?

A) increasing linear

B) decreasing linear

C) increasing exponential

D) decreasing exponential

10. The population of Illinois decreased from 12,830,632 in 2010 to 12,812,508 in 2020. This is approximately a 1.26% decrease in population. If the 2020 population is t times the 2010 population, what is the value of t?

A) 1.0126

B) 0.9874

C) 1.0244

D) 0.9926

11. For the exponential function a, the value of $a(1)$ is p, where p is a constant. Which of the following equivalent forms of the function a shows the value of p as the coefficient or the base?

   A) $144 \times (2.35)^{x-1}$
   B) $126 \times (4.66)^{x}$
   C) $144 \times (2.35)^{x}$
   D) $126 \times (2.35)^{x+1}$

12. Hunter is collecting baseball cards. Each year, he collects 20% more baseball cards than he did the year before. Hunter collected 143 baseball cards in 2021. Which one of the following equations represents how many baseball cards Hunter collected in 2023, where c is the estimated number of baseball cards collected and y represents the number of years that have elapsed since the beginning of Hunter's hobby?

   A) $c = 143 \times (1.2)^{3t}$
   B) $c = 1.2 \times (143)^{t}$
   C) $c = 143 + (1.2)^{t}$
   D) $c = 143 \times (1.2)^{t}$

13. Which expression is equivalent to $u^{8 \div 9}$, where $u > 0$?

   A) $\sqrt[81]{u^{72}}$
   B) $\sqrt[81]{u^{9}}$
   C) $\sqrt[9]{u^{8}}$
   D) $\sqrt[72]{u^{81}}$

14. In the figure shown, line a intersects parallel lines b and c. What is the value of angle z?

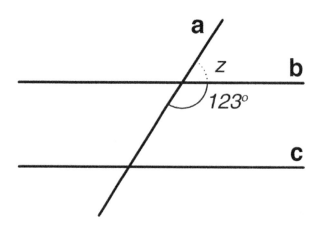

   A)   33 degrees
   B)   123 degrees
   C)   57 degrees
   D)   303 degrees

15. A cube has an edge length of 26 feet. A sphere with a radius of 14 feet is next to the cube. By volume, how much more space does the cube take up than the sphere? Round to the nearest foot.

   A)   3,041 feet
   B)   11,494 feet
   C)   12,164 feet
   D)   6,082 feet

16. The function t is defined by $t(o) = 21o^3$. What is the value of o when $t(o)$ is equal to 1,344?

    A)   3

    B)   4

    C)   5

    D)   6

17. What is the solution to the given equation?

$$12x - 32 = 256$$

18. The x-intercept of the graph shown is $(x, 0)$. What is the value of x?

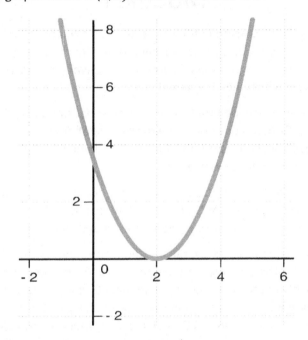

19. The function k is defined by $k(x) = 0.4x + 5$. Which number represents the y-intercept in the function?

20. If $|2x + 8| = 126$, what is the positive value of $x - 2$?

21. Johnathan is buying tickets to a baseball game for his friends. Each ticket to the game costs $25. The ticket website charges a $30 one-time purchasing fee. He also wants to purchase one $5 hot dog for each of his friends while at the game. Johnathan has $180 that he is able to spend on the outing. How many people, *including himself*, can Johnathan afford to bring to the game?

22. $2x^2 + 24x + c = 0$

In the given equation, c is a constant. The equation has no real solutions if $c > n$. What is the LEAST possible value of n?

Answer Key #2
Reading & Writing

Module I

1. C: Option C fits best with the discussion in the rest of the passage about murderers later regretting the deed. Options A and B would require these murders to be regarded positively, with option A requiring the passage not to mention the killers' subsequent downfalls, and option D requiring the murders to be the reasons for which the killers exist.

2. A: Option A best matches with the idea that the protagonist has been told to accept his lot in life and not worry about the results. Option B does not fit with the idea of doing one's duties as described. The "forgetting" in option C does not seem naturally at odds with doing these duties. Since a loss is directly described in the text, option D cannot be correct.

3. B: Option B acknowledges the fact that the sonnet's final couplet is a warning to the subject about being overlooked after death if he does not "get a son." The text does not describe a pilgrimage as in option A, and its main concern is not describing the phases of age, as in options C and D.

4. A: Option A is correct because the sentence talking about the stagnant ponds where country folk can catch eels provides context for the statement that country folk have "queer notions" about where eels come from, which presumably relates to where they are able to find them. The sentence before would need to be unclear for option B to be correct, and there would have to be some contradiction between this sentence and the previous one for option C to be correct. Option D would only work if something were merely implied in the previous sentence when its points have been stated outright.

5. B: Option B correctly sums up the view in Text 2 that respect should be given to animals, which would include cats. Option A states an opinion about people, and we cannot know if the author of Text 2 shares such an opinion. Options C and D do not fit with the entreaty in Text 2 to think more highly of animals.

6. C: Option C fits best with the idea of great public attention. Options A and D would require the theory about to be introduced to have avoided notice, which does not make sense in conjunction with the first sentence. Option B would mean that the scientists found their interest disrupted by this theory.

7. D: Option D correctly identifies the text as a series of thoughts from the protagonist. Option A would require the passage to be telling the story of the fight rather than dwelling on the protagonist's thoughts about it. Options B and C describe a shift from description to reflection and explanation respectively, and no such change takes place in the text

8. B: Option B most effectively sums up the passage's point that the unpretentious and true will be "always beautiful and good." Option A makes a statement about rococo art, and Option D makes a general statement about fashion, neither of which is the subject of the passage. Option C focuses on the idea that "artificial things" will please for a time and then come back into fashion much later, while the passage cares more about the enduring goodness of the unpretentious.

9. A: Option A is the only option that properly follows as a contradiction and fits the idea of the balance between philosophies being discussed. Option B is not a contradiction at all, begging the question of why the "but" statement would be used. Option C does not fit with the idea that all the essays are tacitly, or by implication, evolutionary—this indicates that they are evolutionary enough to show it without the fact being stated outright. Earlier in the sentence, the author directly states that aesthetics are involved in the essays, making option D incorrect.

10. D: Option D shows Lockwood clearly recognizing that Heathcliff does not want to invite him in but thinking that Heathcliff's unhappiness being endearing to him is a good enough reason to impose on him anyway. Option A only shows Lockwood talking and gives no indication of how Heathcliff feels about the interaction. Option B only shows Heathcliff speaking, with no evidence of Lockwood's silliness. Option C shows Lockwood being oblivious about why someone would have chosen to live in a "misanthropist's Heaven" in the first place, but it does not refer to a specific interaction between the man and his unhappy landlord.

11. C: Option C shows that the number of homes sold has fallen overall during the period from 2010 – 2019 by comparing the numbers in those two years. Options A and B only share one number each, which gives no indication of whether the number has risen or fallen overall. Option D only compares data from the first three years shown on the graph, which cannot tell us what happened by the end of 2019.

12. A: Option A supports the fact that building an audience for such plays requires support, and that there is a portion of the public that the passage's author can point to as a source of said support. If Option B were true, the author would not need to make an argument that there is an audience for these plays. If Option C were true, the author would have no leg to stand on, as there would be no audience for them. Option D is a non sequitur in a passage that does not reference cricket.

13. B: Option B notes a decrease in the participants' heightened fight/flight reflex in the experimental group, which would be the result the researchers had hypothesized. Option A would mean that the intervention does nothing. Option C would mean that the intervention is actively harmful because it increased an already heightened fight/flight reflex in participants. Option D would also mean that the intervention is harmful, because only those who did not do the daily "tummy time" showed improvement.

14. C: Option C uses parallel structure in the repeated "the *X* thing is *X*-est" phrases. Options A, B, and D all fail to preserve the parallelism used in the first two phrases.

15. A: In Option A, the nonessential phrase *through contrasts in luminosity* is set off from the rest of the sentence. Options B and C fail to set the phrase off from the rest of the sentence, and option D creates a grammatically incorrect division of phrases with an unnecessary semicolon.

16. D: Option D correctly uses a semicolon to separate a multi-phrase item in the list from the others. Option A lacks necessary punctuation; option B uses an em dash when the next item in the list is separated from the last by a semicolon; and option C uses a comma where a semicolon is required for clarity.

17. B: Option B uses present tense, which matches the rest of the verbs in these two sentences. Options A, C, and D all switch into past tense.

18. A: Option A divides the two sentences properly with a period. Option B would require the first sentence to be phrased like a question, which it is not. Option C would require the second sentence to

be elaborating on the first. Option D creates a run-on sentence by improperly joining two complete sentences.

19. D: Option D makes correct use of the em dash to introduce the next part of the sentence. Option A lacks necessary punctuation. Option B sets off the phrase "and where there are" as if it were a nonessential phrase. Option C cuts off the sentence in a way that separates the phrase "where there are" from the word *among* and makes what follows grammatically awkward.

20. D: Option D reflects the fact that this sentence provides an additional aspect of this change that needs to be explained. Options A, B, and C all require this sentence's statement (that this aspect needs explaining) to contradict the statement in the previous sentence about other aspects that are challenging to imagine.

21. B: Option B reflects the contrast between gentlemanliness and vulgarity. Option A would require that the two to be similar, and option C would require that vulgarity follow gentlemanliness chronologically. Option D would require the second sentence's negative comments about vulgarity to contradict the first sentence's positive comments about gentlemanliness.

22. B: Option B fully explains the etymology of the word *brontosaurus*. Option A mentions the translation of "thunder lizard," but does not explain it. Options C and D share completely different facts about the brontosaurus.

23. A: Option A recognizes that the statement in this sentence logically follows the previous sentence. Options B, C, and D all require this sentence about the artist's act of creation to contradict the other sentences.

24. C: Option C points out the claims of inaccuracy and presents Capote's option to write down quotes by memory as the reason. Option A mentions the claims but then gives Capote credit for the capture of the killers. Option B emphasizes the attention the book received rather than Capote's writing methods, and option D fails to share the method Capote used to take his notes.

25. D: Option D matches best with this sentence, which describes a level of engraving unmatched by those previously mentioned. Options A and B would require these engravings to be extraordinary because there are others that are simply good and bad. Option C would diminish the praise to follow, which does not fit well with such strongly worded praise.

26. C: Option C uses the notes about Callas's nickname and repertoire to emphasize her range and the respect she received as an artist. Option A only implies that Callas sang the work of many composers and gives no real description of her reputation as a singer. Option B places more emphasis on when Callas began her education and her eventual vocal decline than on her complimentary nickname. Option D is all about Callas's temperamental behavior and does a poor job of introducing her as an artist.

27. A: Option A presents Dr. Gray's opinion that the experiment's design actively encouraged the abuse that occurred. Option B states that the fake prisoners were really arrested, but does not give any further information, such as whether this was a normal, acceptable, or agreed-upon part of the experiment. Option C says that the experiment was unethical, but only gives a neutral explanation of the experiment. Option D states an opinion about the possible effect of the weather on the participants' psyches, which is irrelevant to the study and the ethical questions posed.

Module II

1. C: Option C matches best with the humility with which the writer admits to a lack of credentials in the following sentence. Option A would be declaring that there are multiple versions of this work, which the reader has been given no reason to expect. Option B would be praising the work rather than stating a caveat. Option D would mean there were pieces physically sticking out of the work.

2. A: Option A fits most logically with the discussion in the passage of how students are taught in Lamar County. Options B, C, and D are all subjects that would be covered in school, but only option A matches the discussion of how schooling itself is conducted.

3. D: Option D best sums up the passage's purpose in declaring that "the living body is a mechanism." Options A and B would make the opposite argument, and option C would require more emphasis to be placed on the importance of studying these vital processes than on the fact that they are mundane and able to be scientifically explained.

4. B: Option B is correct because this sentence gives the "facts of the matter" of the narrator's death, which the previous sentence indicates will come next. Option A would mean that the first sentence is already discussing the narrator's death and the second sentence is providing more information about it. There is no subject change for option C, and the sentence does nothing to make the idea of the narrator dying and coming back to life less far-fetched, as in option D.

5. D: Option D fits best with the author of Text 1's statement that mysticism could become "a mischievous faculty" if unregulated, which is possible if the concept itself is viewed as detached from the concepts of right and wrong. Option A would mean that the author of Text 1 believes that mysticism is a set of rules rather than a concept that should have rules applied to it. Options B and C would require the author of Text 1 to think that the author of Text 2 is making defamatory statements about mysticism rather than defining one of its doctrines.

6. C: Option C is correct in identifying this as the name the man used in prison. Option A would mean that the man was running a scam he in prison. Option B would mean that the man worked a job at the prison. Option D would mean that the man made a friend in prison.

7. A: Option A is most accurate to the many places and objects the passage describes as being touched by the fog. In option B, the fog would only be a focus in the first part of the passage, and in option C, there would need to be competing descriptions of pleasant and unpleasant sights throughout. We are given no indication that this fog is sentient, as is stated in option D.

8. B: Option B correctly identifies the consistent trend against neutrality as evidenced by the very low percentages in that column of the table. Option A would require the participants to have negative feelings overall toward AI use in navigation, which is not what the table shows. Option C gives an incorrect percentage for how many respondents feel negatively toward AI use in visual art. Option D would only be correct if the responses were consistent in how favorably they viewed AI across all three different uses, which is not the case.

9. C: Option C's emphasis on the book's contribution to the teaching of the subject matches best with the passage's previous statement about the company being glad that it can offer this new book to schools. Option A says that the book is cost prohibitive, and the idea of the book being hard to get is at odds with the passage's talk of making this kind of resource "integral to elementary education." Option B asserting that this book is the only one that can make this claim is at odds with it being "one of the

new types" of books that are like this. Option D asserting that the book is more likely to become obsolete in recent years is at odds with the goals stated for the book in the passage.

10. A: Option A correctly sums up the passage's main point about the differences between tradition and saga. Options B and C are both statements made within the passage, but they do not capture its main idea. Option D makes a false statement about the difference between tradition and saga.

11. D: Option D is the best answer because the passage is entirely focused on the fact that we do not know the identity of the first potter. Options A and B make general statements about potters themselves that state opinions not indicated by the text, and option C is a call to action that the author of the passage never gives.

12. C: Option C shows a participant feeling significantly more stressed by the interviewer's lack of expressiveness. Option A expresses nothing about this interview in particular, and option B expresses enjoyment of the part of the experiment hypothesized to cause increased stress. In option D, the participant expresses only annoyance, not stress.

13. B: Option B is the only option that states another issue that would prevent the author from agreeing with Nicholson's conclusions. Options A, B, and C all involve the author agreeing with Nicholson, which the passage's first sentence explicitly states is not the case.

14. B: Option B recognizes that the first sentence is phrased as a question. Options A, C, and D all fail to present the sentence as a question, with option D also combining the two sentences.

15. D: Option D uses the pronoun *its* to match with the word *itself* in the previous sentence. Options A, B, and C use pronouns for one or more people rather than the correct pronoun *its* for the object "an industrial world."

16. C: Option C sets off the nonessential phrase "after Polybius" from the rest of the sentence. Options A, B, and D all fall short of the two commas necessary to properly set off the phrase.

17. A: Option A uses the plural *phenomena* correctly after the general modifier *certain*. Option B incorrectly uses the singular *phenomenon* after the word *certain*. Option C incorrectly leaves *phenomena* plural after changing the modifier to singular and specific. Option D pluralizes a word that is already plural.

18. D: Option D correctly uses the noun *effect*. Option A uses the verb *affect* incorrectly as a substitute for the noun *effect*. Option B makes the same mistake while also adding an *s* to the end of the word, and option C unnecessarily pluralizes *effect*.

19. A: Option A does not add unnecessary punctuation to the sentence. Option B treats the phrase "who knew much better how not to err" as a nonessential phrase to be set off from the rest of the sentence. Options C and D unnecessarily separate "many men" from "who knew much better how not to err."

20. D: Option D recognizes that this sentence provides an example of the criticism mentioned in the previous sentence. Options A, B, and C all require the sentence to contradict the previous sentence rather than give an example of what it describes.

21. A: Option A recognizes that the previous sentence explains why the air being expelled contains a large proportion of carbonic gas. Option B requires the sentence to contradict what has been explained. Option C requires the expulsion of air to precede the explanation of respiration chronologically, and Option D requires the sentence to provide additional information instead of drawing a conclusion about what has already been shared.

22. B: Option B combines the two notes about the bird's appearance to effectively describe it. Options A, C, and D all give different facts about the bird.

23. A: Option A places the young man's actions chronologically before those of the one in the previous sentence, which makes the most sense with the description of the man having seen the war party's approach rather than having heard the gunshot. Option B would require this man to have met with the war party's approach as a result of the warning, which makes no sense. Option C would require the man to have deliberately been surprised by the war party in response to hearing the warning, which would also make no sense. Option D calls the two men similar, but they had opposite responses to the approaching threat.

24. D: Option D gives full explanations of all three parts without redefining terms the audience is known to be familiar with. Options A and B both fail to explain the three types, with option B also defining a term the audience already knows. Option C only explains the Exiles.

25. B: Option B fits best with the general sending these men despite there being no sign of the enemy. Options A, B, and C only work if sending men to reconnoiter was the expected outcome of seeing no sign of the enemy.

26. C: Option C focuses exclusively on the painting. Options A, B, and C all split focus and emphasize something other than *The Persistence of Memory* painting.

27. C: Option C effectively uses both notes about similarities between Scout's family and Lee's. Option A mentions the two facts about Lee's family that were similar to Scout's family, but it does not mention the corresponding facts about Scout's family. Options B and D share unrelated facts.

Answer Key #2
Math

Module I

1. C: First, the equation 0.5×880 needs to be put in simplest form. The product of the equation is 440, and 5% of 440 is found by multiplying 0.05×440. Thus, 5% of 0.5×880 is 22.

2. B: When dividing the equation $15x - 5 = 100$ by 5, the equation becomes $3x - 1 = 20$, in which x has a value of 7.

3. D: By substituting the value of y into the second equation, it can be simplified to $6x - 4x = 12$. This can be simplified to $2x = 12$, which can be used to determined that $x = 6$.

4. B: The number 84 represents the total dollar amount of merchandise sold. By multiplying the price of items sold and the number of each type of item (x and y), it can be determined that computing $4x + 12y = 84$.

5. D: Using the distributive property, it can be determined that multiplying $(x^2y^3 + 2x + 4y)$ by 2^4 will yield $2x^82y^{12} + 4x^48y^4$.

6. D: By examining the slope of the line (2) and seeing that the y-intercept is 8, it can be determined that the line is represented by $y = 2x + 8$.

7. A: Since the slope of the line of best fit is going downward and the y-intercept seems to be somewhere around 5.5, the line of best fit would most likely be represented by $y = -1.6x + 5.48$.

8. D: Use the formula for the area of a circle and insert the radius to determine that Circle A is represented by $\pi(2n)^2$ and Circle B is represented by $\pi(124n)^2$. These simplify to $4\pi n$ and $15,376\pi n$. Dividing the area of Circle B by the value of Circle A's area demonstrates that the area of Circle B is 3,844 times larger than the area of Circle A.

9. B: To find the area of the park in square yards, first find the squared value of however many yards are in a mile (3,097,600), and then multiply that value by the number of square miles in the park (234). The product is 724,838,400 miles.

10. C: The measure of angle J is equal to $2\pi \div 4 + 4\pi \div 16$. In order to gain a common denominator, multiply the measure of angle P by 4 to yield $8\pi \div 16$. When added to the second equation, the measure of angle J can be said to be $12\pi \div 16$ radians, which can be simplified to $3\pi \div 4$ radians. In order to find the measure of angle J in degrees, multiply $3\pi \div 4$ by $180 \div \pi$. This yields 135 degrees.

11. B: Since Jonathan's budget is $700, he can spend a maximum of $200 on bags of food after paying the fixed $500 adoption fee. The total food cost would be represented by the per-bag price of $20 multiplied by the number of bags. Thus, the inequality that best represents Johnathan's budget is $20b + 500 \leq 700$.

12. B: Since angles L and P are congruent, they must add up to 90. Thus, the measure of angle P is 44°.

13. A: Since x is multiplied by the number of aisles in the store and y is multiplied by the number of display cases in the store, multiplying the number of products per aisle and the number of products per display case by the total number of aisles and display cases would yield 4,556 total products. Thus, the value of y represents the number of products per display case in the store.

14. B: Although there is one data value represented by 4 that occurs 9 times, more than any others, there are two data values represented by 5 that have a combined frequency of 10.

15. A: Since each letter of the alphabet is represented by 2 names in the drawing, the first 7 letters of the alphabet are represented by 14 entrants. The probability of both names starting with the first 7 letters of the alphabet is $\frac{2}{14}$, which is $\frac{1}{7}$ in simplified form.

16. D: By plugging in each choice for x and utilizing the trial-and-error method, the order of operations can determine that $2(8^2) - 7 = 121$. Therefore, the value of x when $m(x) = 121$ is 8.

17. Using the equation provided, it can be determined that the point at the center of the circle is represented by coordinates $(4, 6)$. The endpoints are provided. The value of r can be found by plugging the coordinates of the circle's center and one endpoint into the distance formula, which is represented by $\sqrt{(x_1 - x_2)^2 + (y_1 - y_2)^2}$. By computing for $\sqrt{(4 - 3)^2 + (6 - 4)^2}$, which is simplified into $\sqrt{1^2 + 2^2}$, it can be determined that **r is equivalent to 3**.

b The inequality in this situation is represented by the fixed cost of the car ($15,000); the fixed cost of gas; oil changes; and maintenance ($900 multiplied by the number of years, y); and the cost of upgrades (z). These fixed costs and variables have to be less than or equal to $18,250, which is Kevin's maximum budget. Since Kevin has only owned the car for one year, he has only spent $15,900 thus far. In order to find the maximum value of z, subtract $15,900 from $18,250. This yields **$2,350** left over that Kevin is able to spend on upgrades.

19. The system can be solved for y using the method of substitution. Since the first equation already isolated the value of x, it can be plugged into the second equation to find y. The second equation becomes $(6 \times 4y) - 2y = 66$, which can be simplified to $22y = 66$. Once both sides are divided by 22, it can be said that **$y = 3$**.

20. Since the country's population doubles every 20 years at a constant rate, it can also be estimated that the population increases by 50% every 10 years. Multiplying 3,500,000 by 2 shows that the population in 2030 will be 7,000,000. Multiplying 7,000,000 by 2 demonstrates that the population in 2050 will be 14,000,000. Since the objective is to find the population only 10 years after 2050 instead of 20, multiplying 14,000,000 by 1.5 will yield a likely total population of **21,000,000 people** in 2060.

21. Since pants are on the y-axis, the y-intercept can be found by identifying the maximum number of pants that Tom can purchase (9). Since each shirt is half the cost of each pair of pants, and each shirt purchased removes half of Tom's ability to purchase a single pair of pants, the **slope of the line is -0.5**.

22. First, the slope of line J must be found: $(145 - 122) \div (22 - 16)$ yields a slope of 4. The line's slope equation is $y = 4x + b$. By using the line's slope and plugging in an (x, y) coordinate into slope-intercept form ($y = mx + b$), the equation $122 = (4 \times 16) + b$ can be created. Simplifying and solving shows that $b = 58$. Substituting the value of b back into the line's slope equation yields $y = 4x + 58$. Since line P is translated 6 units up from line J, its equation is represented by $y = 4x + 64$. When substituting 0 for y, the equation yields $0 = 4x + 64$. When solving for x, the equation yields a value of -16. Therefore, line **P crosses the x-axis at -16**.

Module II

1. B: Multiply the number of hours that Jane works (24) by her hourly rate of h to find her total income d. Thus, $24h = d$ will yield Jane's total income from 24 hours of work.

2. A: By plugging in the values provided, the equation becomes $30 = 240 \div g$. By solving for g, it can be determined that the sedan used 8 gallons to travel 240 miles at an efficiency rate of 30 miles per gallon.

3. C: By plugging the values of a and b into the Pythagorean Theorem ($a^2 + b^2 = c^2$), it can be determined that the value of c would be equal to the square root of the sum of a and b.

4. C: Use knowledge of slope-intercept form ($y = mx + b$) to determine that since the value of the y-intercept in the equation (b) is -3, the y-intercept of the line must be at grid coordinate $(0, -3)$.

5. A: By simplifying the equation, it can be determined that $4x^2 - (-5x^2)$ becomes an addition problem equaling $9x^2$ due to two subtraction signs canceling one another out. The second half of the problem, $8x + (-2x)$ subtracts to become $6x$. Therefore, the equivalent expression is $9x^2 + 6x$.

6. D: Use mental math in the first equation to determine that $x = 10$. Furthermore, the first equation is present inside of the second. To solve for y, plug in the value of x to yield $(20 + 4)^2 = 4y$. Once the equation is simplified to $576 = 4y$, dividing both sides by 4 yields 144 for the value of y. Therefore, the ordered pair that fits is $(10, 144)$.

7. D: Add all data values together to yield the sum of 65. Divide this number by the data values (13) to find the mean average of 5.

8. B: Since the purpose of a function is to substitute various numbers for the value of x, the minimum value that can be inserted in the place of x is 0. Thus, since $0^3 = 0$, $0 + 23$ yields a minimum value of 23 for the function.

9. C: Since Henry's account gains value based upon however much it is worth during the year that it increases, rather than only increasing based upon its starting value, Henry's investment changes over time are an example of compounding interest, which is an increasing exponential function.

10. B: Since the percentage of Illinoisans decreased by 1.26%, finding the value of 98.74% of the 2010 population will yield the 2020 population. In decimal form, 98.74% is represented as 0.9874.

11. A: Take into account the value of the exponent attached to 2.35: 2.35^{1-1} equals 1. Thus, 144×1 is 144, and $p = 144$, which is the coefficient of the equation.

12. D: In the equation, 143 is the base of the equation since it was the number of cards Hunter started out with. In order to represent the number of cards Hunter has in 2023, 143 should be multiplied by a decimal representing the 20% increase in the amount of cards Hunter has to the power of however many years Hunter has been collecting, which ends up being $(1.2)^t$ in the equation.

13. A: Multiplying the exponent of the original expression by $9 \div 9$ yields $u^{(8 \div 9) \times (9 \div 9)}$. Simplified, that equals $u^{72 \div 81}$. By modulating this equation as $(u^{72})^{1 \div 81}$, it can be determined that the equivalent expression is $\sqrt[81]{u^{72}}$.

14. C: Angle z is complementary to the angle that is already labeled with a degree value. Subtract to find the measurement of angle z: $180 - 123$ yields a value of 57 degrees.

15. D: First, the volume of the cube must be found using the formula $v = s^3$. 26^3 is equivalent to 17,576 feet. Second, the volume of the sphere must be found using the formula $v = (4 \div 3)\pi r^3$. Plug the

sphere's radius into the equation as $v = (4 \div 3)\pi(14)^3$. The volume of the sphere is 11,494.04 feet (rounded to 11,494). To determine the size disparity between the two shapes, subtract 11,494 from 17,576 to yield a difference of 6,082 feet.

16. B: To solve the equation algebraically, begin by dividing both sides by 21 to yield $64 = o^3$, and then find the cubed root of both sides to yield $4 = o$. Thus, the value of o when $t(o) = 1{,}344$ is 4.

17. First, isolate the variable by adding 32 to each side, which yields $12x = 288$. Then, divide both sides by 12 to yield $x = 24$.

18. Because the midpoint of the parabola touches down at grid coordinate $(2, 0)$, the value of x is 2.

19. Because the function k's equation is in slope-intercept form, it can be determined that the y-intercept (b in the equation) has a value of 5.

20. First, both the positive and negative values of the absolute value equation must be found: $2x + 8 = 126$ and $-2x - 8 = 126$ can be computed to find values of 59 and -67, respectively. Then, use both numbers to find the values of $x - 2$. $59 - 2 = 57$ and $-67 - 2 = -69$. The sum of these two numbers will produce the positive value of $x - 2$, which is -12.

21. Since each attendee will have one ticket and one hot dog, the total price per person is $30. The total amount of people that can attend the game is represented by the equation $30x + 30 = 180$. Subtract 30 from each side of the equation, leaving $30x = 150$. Divide each side by 30 to yield $x = 5$. Thus, including himself, Johnathan can bring 5 people to the baseball game.

22. First, identify which numbers correspond to which variables in the quadratic equation. In this instance, $a = 2$, $b = 24$, and c is still unknown. Use the discriminant equation for imaginary numbers $b^2 - 4ac < 0$ to find the maximum number that n can be while still being less than the value of c. By plugging in the values previously mentioned into the discriminant equation, $24^2 - 4 \times (2) \times (c) < 0$ yields $576 - 8c < 0$. Subtracting 576 from both sides results in $-8c < -576$. When dividing both sides by -8, the less-than sign is reversed and the equation yields $c > 72$. Therefore, the least possible value of n is 72.

ONLINE RESOURCES

Trivium includes online resources with the purchase of this study guide to help you fully prepare for the exam.

Review Questions

Need more practice? Our review questions use a variety of formats to help you memorize key terms and concepts.

Flash Cards

Trivium's flash cards allow you to review important terms easily on your computer or smartphone.

Cheat Sheets

Review the core skills you need to master the exam with easy-to-read Cheat Sheets.

From Stress to Success

Watch "From Stress to Success," a brief but insightful YouTube video that offers the tips, tricks, and secrets experts use to score higher on the exam.

Feedback

Let us know what you think!

Access these materials at: acceptedinc.com/sat-online-resources

Dear SAT test taker,

Great job completing this study guide. The hard work and effort you put into your test preparation will help you succeed on your upcoming SAT exam. Thank you for letting us be a part of your education journey!

We have other study guides and products that you may find useful. Search for us on Amazon.com or let us know what you are looking for. We offer a wide variety of study guides that cover a multitude of subjects.

If you would like to share your success stories with us, or if you have a suggestion, comment, or concern, please send us an email at support@triviumtestprep.com.

Thanks again for choosing us!
Happy Testing
Trivium Test Prep Team

Made in the USA
Coppell, TX
26 August 2024

36472822R00109